# A CITY OF PALACES

Richard Grainger and the Making of Newcastle upon Tyne

# A City of Palaces

Richard Grainger and the Making of Newcastle upon Tyne

*"You walk into what has long been termed the COAL HOLE OF THE NORTH
and find yourself at once in A CITY OF PALACES; a fairyland of newness,
brightness and modern elegance. And who has wrought this change?
It is Mr Grainger."*

(W. Howitt, 1842[1])

## Ian Ayris

Newcastle Libraries & Information Service

# Acknowledgements

Acknowledgements are notoriously dull and go mostly unread, but as the amount of research a literature on the history and heritage of Newcastle grows it is difficult to publish anything, matter how humble, which does not owe a great debt to those who have gone before. Of Rich Grainger there is still more to be said – but even that which is said here owes much to the publish works of, initially, Lyall Wilkes and Gordon Dodds, and latterly Tom Faulkner and his colleagues – leading contemporary authorities on this most important period in the development of Newcast Placing these events in a wider historical and social context has placed further reliance on the works prominent historians – notably those of Asa Briggs, David Lowenthal and Raymond Williams – all whom are, I hope, correctly accredited. Most credit is however due to the combined expertise of parts the City of Newcastle Planning Department, in particular the Tyne and Wear Specialist Conservati Team, the Environmental Design Team, and the Graingertown Project Team, especially Peter Howe a David Lovie; the Laing Art Gallery (Tyne & Wear Museums) and the Local Studies and Studio person of the City Library. Particular mention is due to Ruth Trotter and Patricia Sheldon for illustrative a documentary references, Wilma Ayris for meticulous proofreading and Anna Flowers for her skills in formulation and design of this publication.

*A City of Palaces* is published to mark the bicentenary of the birth of Richard Grainger. Its publicati has been generously supported by English Partnerships.

Ian Ayris is a member of the Tyne and Wear Specialist Conservation Team based in the Planni Department of the City of Newcastle upon Tyne.

Illustrations are copyright of Newcastle upon Tyne City Library, except for the following. Photograp on pages 33, 73, 82, and 83 are copyright of Dave Hewitt, and that on page 74 is copyright of Dr To Yellowley. The front cover picture and those on pages 2, 14, 20, 28, 36, 39, 42, 49, 62, 63, 67 and 72 a reproduced by kind permission of the Laing Art Gallery, Tyne & Wear Museums. The back cov photograph is copyright of City Repro.

Many of the engravings are reproduced from *Architectural and Picturesque Views in Newcastle up Tyne*, by W. Collard and M. Ross, 1841.

Incidental illustrations are taken from *A Glossary of Terms used in Gothic Architecture*, 1850, and 18 *Woodcuts by Thomas Bewick and his School*, 1962, and other sources in Newcastle City Library.

Front cover and page 2:
Richard Grainger (1797-1861) Artist unknown, c.1830, Laing Art Gallery

Cover design by A.V. Flowers

City of Newcastle upon Tyne
Community & Leisure Services Department
Newcastle Libraries & Arts, 1997

ISBN: 1 85795 063 1

Cataloguing-in-Publication data. A catalogue record for this book is available from the British Library.

Printed by Bailes the Printer, Houghton-le-Spring

# Contents

| | Introduction | 7 |
|---|---|---|
| Chapter 1 | An Atmosphere of Rampant Change | 9 |
| Chapter 2 | Rattling, Growling, Smoking, Stinking | 13 |
| Chapter 3 | Newcastle is Peru | 16 |
| Chapter 3 | All Things Connect | 20 |
| Chapter 5 | A Vast Quantity of Ground | 27 |
| Chapter 6 | A Raw Lad like Grainger | 31 |
| Chapter 7 | The Pride of the Town | 35 |
| Chapter 8 | Mr Grainger Acts | 40 |
| Chapter 9 | The Extraordinary Magician | 45 |
| Chapter 10 | Lofty and Modern Mansions | 53 |
| Chapter 11 | The Link Snaps | 59 |
| Chapter 12 | The Genius of Richard Grainger | 67 |
| Chapter 13 | Grainger Town | 75 |
| | Notes | 84 |
| | Index | 87 |

**The Grey Monument, c.1841, engraved by William Collard**

**From *Architectural and Picturesque Views in Newcastle upon Tyne* by W. Collard and M. Ross, 1841.**

"Our view of this magnificent column is taken from the corner of Hood Street, and embraces the termination of Grey Street and Grainger Street, and a portion of Blackett Street."

Richard Grainger, builder, developer, entrepreneur, left his eloquent signature on the history and the streets of Newcastle upon Tyne.

# Introduction

In 1854, late in his life, Richard Grainger was asked to summarise the number of new houses and streets he had built in Newcastle; he replied:

"A great many ... I have built part of New Bridge Street, Carliol Street... Croft Street, Portland Place, Northumberland Street ... 31 houses in Blackett Street, 22 in Eldon Square, three in Newgate Street, nine in Percy Street, 68 in Leazes Terrace, 80 in Leazes Crescent and other streets adjoining; 14 in St James' Street and Terrace, the whole of the Royal Arcade ... used as the post office and shops, the excise office and the bankruptcy courts ... and two banks. Grey Street I built entirely, 81 houses, Market Street, the whole, consisting of 38 houses; Grainger Street, 68 houses; Nun's Street, the whole, 26 houses, Nelson Street, the same number, 26 houses; Clayton Street, 107 the whole; Clayton Street West, 27, the whole, Hood Street, 16, the whole; Shakespeare Street, the whole, 16; Pilgrim Street, a part, 14; Nun's Gate, six, a part; Rye Hill, 23; Elswick, 19, Railway Street, 20 ..."[1]

Richard Grainger (1797-1861), builder, developer and entrepreneur, was without doubt the single most important influence on the development of central Newcastle in the nineteenth century. "Few men have accomplished so much as he by way of improving the physical aspect of their native town" observed the writer Lawson.[2] His contribution to the making of the town was unique; he changed the appearance, the nature, the commercial heart and the external perception of Newcastle. He gave a nucleus to the developing conurbation from which a great Victorian city grew. The changes he wrought in Newcastle from 1820 to 1840 were a product of his own work, vision and abilities but they were also forged by, and were symptomatic of, the age in which he lived. For change was the principal characteristic of the decades which followed the twenty years of war against Revolutionary and Napoleonic France which ended at Waterloo in 1815. These were perhaps the most important years in the industrial, political, commercial and social history of modern Britain.

Change by its nature is however not spontaneous. There were many factors and events which influenced the transformation which Grainger brought about, which made the time and the climate right for the redevelopment of the still predominantly medieval town of Newcastle. This was an age of individual enterprise and of professional men, creating a new

**Richard Grainger c.1839**

The buildings of Grey Street form a backdrop to a portrait of Richard Grainger – the Northumbrian Vitruvius – his finger poised on the plan for the development of Newcastle, symbolising his role as both visionary and builder. Grainger was probably in his early forties when this portrait was painted and was at the height of his career and achievements.

economic culture, of which Richard Grainger was a part. Richard Grainger story is one of singular vision and enterprise but it is also one of time, pla and culture, its central theme is change, and its culmination is the making Newcastle upon Tyne.

# 1 An Atmosphere of Rampant Change

The life of Richard Grainger spanned a period when the pace of industrial, economic and social change, at both a local and national level, accelerated at a previously unknown and unimaginable rate. Most importantly, it was a time when the country changed from a predominantly rural to a predominantly urban based society. Many towns were transformed from medieval market centres to the recognisable conurbations of modern Britain. By the end of the nineteenth century the character, size and importance of our present-day towns and cities were, to a large extent, established. Pinpointing when this process began is as difficult and subjective as determining the origins of the industrial revolution – with which it is inextricably interlinked.

Each generation believes it has lived through a period of considerable change and progress. Looking back with nostalgia to a time when society was less intensely urban, when the pace of life moved with the "timeless rhythms of agriculture and the seasons" has been a popular theme for hundreds of years.[1] Even in the eighteenth century the essayist and playwright Oliver Goldsmith wrung his hands at the loss of rural values – his "sweet Auburn, loveliest village of the plain, where health and plenty cheered the labouring swain" was giving way to the town where "tumultuous grandeur crowds the blazing square, the rattling chariots clash, the torches glare."[2] The same theme is found in the novels of Thomas Hardy, a century later.[3] Writing of the 1830s he charts what he saw as critical changes in

**Newcastle during the Reign of Queen Elizabeth**

An imaginative view of the medieval town by the Newcastle born painter John Storey (1828-1888) which emphasises both the compact riverside nature of the settlement and the steeply rising, deeply incised terrain upon which the town was later to grow.

Port of Tyne Authority

English society, the inherent goodness of rural life being corrupted continually by the evils of the growing towns and the differing mores of the day. This same subject also lies at the heart of George Eliot's *Mill on the Floss* written in 1860 but choosing the England of the 1830s as the time at which this process was at its most poignant.[4] Certainly the period from 1820 when Richard Grainger began to make his mark on Newcastle, until 1861 when he died (and in particular the period to 1840 when he was at his most prolific), saw the transformation not only of Newcastle but of the country as a whole.

At the hub of the emerging industrial nation was the rapidly increasing population. In 1801 the population of the country was in the region of nine million. In the first half of the nineteenth century this figure doubled. Crucially the population not only increased but also migrated within the country to the point where, by the middle of the nineteenth century, the urban population of England for the first time exceeded that of the rural population. In 1800 there were no towns outside of London with a population of 100,000; by 1837 when Queen Victoria came to the throne, there were already five.[5]

The principal forces at work on the social fabric of the country, shaping many of the attitudes and views of the nation, were partly political and partly economic. The example of the French Revolution hovered, like the sword of Damocles, over an unreformed political system and discontent found an outlet in the reform movements of the 1820s and 1830s. The pace of change however, lay fundamentally with the almost uncontrollable speed of the expansion of the extractive and manufacturing industries, led in towns like Manchester, Bradford and Leeds by the textile industry and in the North East of England by the coal industry. As one commentator observed, "the face of the country and the lives of most of its inhabitants seemed transformed beyond recognition and, for many, beyond redemption."[6]

**Lemington Iron Works on the Tyne, 1835**

The fiery furnace was an apocalyptic – almost satanic – image of industry. The heat, fire and smoke of the Tyne Iron Works, founded in 1797, is supplemented by the glow of the High Cone of the Northumberland Glass Works, founded in 1787. Glass manufacture on Tyneside was second only to coal in its importance to the local economy for almost two centuries and was a significant factor in the early industrial development of Newcastle.

Economic fluctuations, with attendant periods of recession, depression, recovery and boom were as common in the first half of the nineteenth century as they are today.[7] Even ten years into the reign of Victoria, as Britain became the world's leading industrial country, the national economy was blighted by the combined failure of the harvest and the Irish potato famine. "What was happening at Westminster or in the City was of small account compared to what was happening in the heavens" observed T. S. Ashton.[8] However, different factors began to play upon the economy as the century wore on. The 1847 harvest crisis was the last. Hand in hand with the move of the population to the urban centres, agriculture lost its hold as the dominant force in the British economy. By 1851 although agricultural work, along with domestic service, was still the largest employer of people in the country, the construction industry had moved into second place. The census of that year included over 440,000 building craftsmen and a further 367,000 general labourers.[9] Certainly the construction industry as a whole, (although by no means as homogeneous as it has become in the late twentieth century), and individual developers, like Grainger, were as prey to economic forces and cycles as they are today. At the beginning of Grainger's career as a builder, construction received a great boost when interest rates fell following the end of the Napoleonic War. The link between interest rates and the building industry is still well established. The decades of peace after 1815 allowed an overall period of prosperity and expansion in building, from which Richard Grainger was to benefit.

Hand in hand with such social and economic upheaval came new requirements, concerns, and opportunities. The Municipal Reform Act of 1835 which reorganised the forms of local government in 263 towns and cities, led to widely diverging interpretations of the role of the local authority from, rarely, guardians of the public health to, more commonly, guardians of the public purse. Whatever approach was taken, however, the first half of the nineteenth century saw the development of a less hidebound form of municipal government. By the 1860s local authorities were beginning to accept the elements of public and social responsibility upon which the traditions of municipal government developed in the later decades of the century. In the years before and immediately after the Reform Act, however, the loosely governed and rapidly expanding towns of the world's leading industrial nation provided extensive opportunities for development. At one extreme these developments could be laudable, durable and highly significant, like the work of Grainger, and at the other, unscrupulous, transitory and ultimately regressive, such as the new housing "estates" of the early Victorian period which fostered the cholera outbreaks of 1848 and 1853 in both Newcastle and Gateshead.[10]

In some respects the early 'Victorian' thrived in the atmosphere of rampant change. The transparent achievements of the period, epitomised by the monuments to a transport revolution – the canals, railways and bridges –

bred a confidence, not to say arrogance, and self-belief which fostered men like Grainger. "No other society had so rapidly embraced invention and innovation or seen its everyday landscapes so thoroughly altered" says historian David Lowenthal.[11] The not unsurprising reaction to the hectic pace of change was one of confusion, epitomised not just by the general disorder of the developing towns, but also in the soul of the nation through its art, architecture and literature. Nowhere was this more evident than in the architecture of the period. In literature, also, great changes took place – the years around 1830 saw the death of William Blake, Sir Walter Scott, Samuel Taylor Coleridge and the high point of the career of Wordsworth.[12] At the same time, however, some of the great names of Victorian literature began to write their first works – Tennyson, Browning and, significantly, in 1835 Charles Dickens. A nation which, in the opening decades of the century enjoyed above all the chivalric historical novels of Sir Walter Scott, was by the 1850s reading the contemporary and metropolitan works of Charles Dickens.

In every way, then, the decades through which Richard Grainger strode, at times like a Colossus, were characterised by change, not least in the rise development and appearance of what are still our major English towns and cities.

**Newcastle upon Tyne by J.M.W. Turner published as part of *Rivers of England*, June 1823**

Viewed from the ballast hills above the North Shore the town and its skyline are dominated still by the medieval symbols of church and state. On the horizon, however, a monument to industry in the form of the shot tower of Elswick Lead Works – established in 1778 – challenges the old order.

# 2

# Rattling, Growling, Smoking, Stinking

Britain's great industrial and manufacturing cities largely grew up on the economic foundations laid in the industrial revolution, their importance and identities fashioned in the atmosphere of rampant change.[1] Those which became regional commercial centres have retained their dominant positions to this day, others, perhaps over-dependent on single industries, have been forced to seek new economic bases to maintain their role and their prosperity. The roll-call of Britain's leading conurbations is taken every week when the successes and failures of their sports teams are read to the nation, their names and status, like the sea areas of the shipping forecast, a familiar litany. In as much as the might and power of our metropolitan centres is reflected in the success of their teams, there lies here a whole history of the urban development of the country. Newcastle, Manchester, Leeds, Liverpool, London and Birmingham clubs dominate the football league tables as they dominate the regions of England. Smaller towns and cities vie for entry into the big league and some have been left behind in the third division. This pattern is very much one forged in the melting pot years of the first half of the nineteenth century.

Some observers saw the growth of these centres as a uniform experience, the effect of industrialisation being to standardise not only all our major towns and cities – Manchester, Leeds etc. but also European and American towns undergoing the same process such as Essen and Youngstown.[2] Others believe the main effect was to differentiate the communities. Certainly the street patterns of Newcastle which grew up in the second half of the nineteenth century bore a stark resemblance to those of other major industrial towns. However, the work which Richard Grainger would carry out ensured that the development of the centre of Newcastle in the first half of the century was unique.

The speed of the development and expansion of many towns took the breath away. Between 1821 and 1831 the population of Manchester increased by 44.9 per cent, that of Leeds by 47.3 per cent, that of Bradford by 65.5 per cent, that of Liverpool by 45.8 per cent.[3] The driving forces which shaped this ostentatious growth varied throughout the country; the textile trades, the railways, the steam engine, the increasingly efficient exploitation of coal, the growth of the steel industry. Completely new towns emerged – Middlesbrough in 1801, for example, contained only four houses and twenty-five inhabitants. Some grew like Topsy – there was only one mill

**The Bigg Market and St Nicholas' Spire, by Thomas Miles Richardson Snr**

The market as the focal point of commercial activity in the town was threatened by the increasing availability and range of manufactured goods. Industrial and commercial development undermined the traditional role of the markets, tied as they were, to predominantly agricultural produce. Their often ramshackle appearance and their blockage of increasingly busy roads were also causes of growing concern to the towns themselves.

Laing Art Gallery

in Bradford in 1801, by 1841 there were 67.[4] Others changed their character Newcastle saw not only the transformation of the town centre but also, like Manchester, the extensive conversion of buildings and areas of the town to warehousing and mercantile establishments.

However, while towns like Newcastle thrived, others slipped behind. In Yorkshire, for example, whilst Leeds and Bradford saw headlong growth, the old market towns of York and Wakefield stagnated. Old ports such as Bristol declined, whilst the Tyne, Wear, Mersey and Thames ports became ever busier. Ancient centres like Lincoln and Norwich, whilst retaining status moved at a sluggish pace. "They passed not so much into eclipse as into torpor, bells ringing, clocks striking, men drinking, women talking and children dancing eternally."[5] That the older towns did not join the economic bandwagon did not preserve them from the problems of health, housing public order and sanitation which came to be associated with industrial centres. Indeed many of the older medieval towns were home to some of the worst conditions of the age. As early as 1799 Robert Southey could say of Exeter, a town which shared many characteristics with Newcastle, that it was "ancient and stinks."[6]

Whilst some, like Joseph Cowen came to recognise the underlying prosperity inherent in the burgeoning communities, the general perception of towns and cities was of dirt and disorder, a necessary evil to be endured rather than adored.[7] John Ruskin saw London as "a great foul city ... rattling

sign of the changing
ture of Newcastle,
the decline of The
lose and the
ayside, and of the
owing demand for
erside storage was
e conversion of the
wn's Mansion
ouse to a warehouse.
uilt in 1691-2 as the
ayor's residence and
e venue for
aborate eighteenth
ntury dinners and
lls, it was
andoned in 1835
d used as a
arehouse until it was
stroyed by fire in
95.

MANSION HOUSE.

growling, smoking, stinking – a ghastly heap of fermenting brickwork, pouring out poison at every pore."[8] Manchester was described as "abominably filthy ... the water of the river as black as ink or the Stygian lake."[9] In a comment comparing English and American attitudes, one commentator observed that "the best society of Philadelphia was trying to improve and glorify Philadelphia, the best society of Manchester was trying to get out of it."

Richard Grainger would buck against this trend. The medieval areas of Newcastle became fever dens and the massive industrial expansion of the second half of the century fostered many of the worst excesses of the Victorian city. However, Grainger's work improved and glorified the town, long before, in other parts of the country, municipal corporations, driven by civic pride, began their processes of aggrandisement. The Newcastle upon which Richard Grainger was to have such a great influence was a town which was facing the cumulative strains of increasing population and increasing industrialisation but in many ways was still waiting to be drawn out of its medieval background.

# 3 Newcastle is Peru

*England's a perfect world; has Indies too*
*Correct your maps: Newcastle is Peru*

(John Cleveland, 1653)

Unlike many of the towns and cities which became nationa[l]
important in the nineteenth century, Newcastle had been a town
consequence since late medieval times. The coal trade broug[ht]
national standing to the town and prosperity to some of its inhabitan[ts].
Indeed, before the rise of the nineteenth century cities, Newcastle vied w[i]
Bristol as the most important town outside of London. As the capital of t[he]
coalfield its importance and influence grew with the expanding coal trad[e].
The shipment of coal from the Tyne grew from an annual total of arou[nd]
15,000 tons in the sixteenth century to over 600,000 tons in 1730-31. Wh[en]
technological development allowed the opening out of the deeper seams
the late eighteenth and early nineteenth centuries this figure leapt agai[n].
Newcastle, however, as the Age of Grainger dawned, was not a mining b[ut]
an increasingly commercial town. The continuing development of t[he]
waggonway allowed the exploitation of reserves at increasing distances fro[m]
the town and the river. Advances in pumping and ventilation led to t[he]
expansion of the coalfield beyond the Ninety Fathom Dyke into South E[ast]
Northumberland, whilst the critically important sinking of Hetton Collie[ry]
presaged the wholesale exploitation of coal beneath the magnesian limesto[ne]
plateau of Durham. As a consequence the flood of coal to the banks of t[he]
Tyne and the Wear became a torrent.[1] The opening of the coal handli[ng]
facilities at firstly the Northumberland Dock, and later the Albert Edwa[rd]
and Tyne Docks, would in time further reduce the direct link between t[he]
town and its most famous export. Meanwhile the manufacturing a[nd]
engineering industries which grew up with the coal trade flourished. Gla[ss]
salt, iron-making and later pottery formed the early basis of the tow[n's]
manufacturing industry.[2] This was later overlaid by the econom[ic]
reinforcements of the chemical industry, which itself grew out of the co[al]
industry, and by the engineering and shipbuilding industries which form[ed]
the other sides of the important industrial triangle based on "carbonifero[us]
capitalism".[3]

As the links between the newly developing outlying mining villages a[nd]
the town of Newcastle grew, its role as the regional capital developed. Th[is]
was, in many ways, a new concept. Other towns such as Manchester a[lso]
became the business capitals of the surrounding constellation of towns a[nd]
villages. As the orbit of these major provincial centres grew, so did the[ir]
importance.[4]

Power and influence within the growing town revolved around the ownership of land and coal, and the workings of the coal trade. In the eighteenth century, the super-wealthy moved out to mansions built on the profits of the trade, such as Gibside or Axwell Park, or indeed to their London homes.[5] Other prominent Newcastle families such as the Ridleys turned their attention to the good husbandry and exploitation of their large country estates in the manner of the leading agricultural improvers of the day.[6] As the century wore on the dominant figures in the town became the growing class of professionals, lawyers, mining engineers, agents and the like. Their position was reflected and bolstered by the development of learned societies, notably the Literary and Philosophical Society which was established in 1793. The personalities who were to play the leading roles in the redevelopment of Newcastle in the early nineteenth century were part of this class – architects, surveyors, builders and solicitors.

The other prime mover in the growing town was the Corporation. In what were still relatively small towns small groups of men were able to control many local activities, acting as town councillors, magistrates and poor law guardians. As a result considerable power was often strongly entrenched in local oligarchies.[7] The 1835 Municipal Reform Act would change, but not revolutionise, either this situation or the functions of local government. In some towns it signalled a transfer of power, in others little changed. For many the role of local government was perhaps encapsulated by the observation made by the first new mayor of the town of Derby, who

**The Quayside in 1745, from a view by R.J. Buck**

By the mid-eighteenth century Newcastle was still largely cocooned within its protective walls. The commercial artery was the river and the heart of the town was the quayside. Movement along the quay was still hampered by the Town Wall but the level of shipping activity east of the medieval Tyne Bridge was prodigious.

observed that the Council's duty was first to establish an efficient pol force and second to be as economical as possible.[8] Indeed many of problems of the old towns were beyond the scope of local government. T social conditions of towns like Exeter and the declining status a importance of older ports like Bristol left local authorities powerless to arr the decline. Perhaps conscious of the plight of the latter town, Newcas Corporation expended its principal efforts on the continuing expansion trade, which through the nineteenth century manifested itself in Corporation's one heroic achievement – the continually extendi quayside.[9]

The Corporation's enthusiasm for commerce often ran contrary to requirements of public hygiene. In 1839, for example, the Corporation s no reason to prevent the manufacture of alkali on the quay area.[10] T magazine *The Builder* observed that "with their mercantile success and ga and eagerness still further to enrich themselves the people of Newcastle ha … utterly neglected all provision for their health."[11] Newcastle was proba the only borough in England and Wales inspected by the General Board Health without the request, blessing or co-operation of the local author Perhaps the blame should not be laid at the door of the Corporation – o 130 signatures could be secured asking for a Board inspection, from a to number of 12000 ratepayers.[12] Similarly Newcastle was not at the forefr in the provision of domestic water supply. A commission, looking at water supply of fifty large towns found Newcastle to be amongst the wo in the Kingdom, eleven houses out of twelve having no water supply.[13] It was also one of the worst lit towns in the country.[14] In some places conditions and facilities beggared belief. In Castle Garth Stairs, for example, 200 or more tenements had the use of only one public 'netty' in a railway arch – "a large open cesspool, over which was thrown a rail, upon which the frequenters support themselves in a row on closest proximity, much in the same style as birds at a roost." In the yards and gardens of the medieval streets the conversion of outhouses for human habitation, known as privy accommodation, plumbed new depths of squalor.[15] The Corporation, meanwhile, gave themselves increasing numbers of powers to improve the town. In 1786 for example an act was passed providing for the cleaning of streets and footpaths, the removal of projections and the building of new streets – but these were predominantly unfulfilled aspirations. The Corporation's eyes were fixed determinedly on the maintenance not of the town but of its trade.

In many ways, then, the Newcastle in which Richard Grainger grew up was a mixture of medieval conditions and of industrial and commercial expansion. In national standing it was perhaps being overtaken by the exploding textile and manufacturing towns, but internally and regionally it was becoming increasingly large and increasingly important. This was only just beginning to be mirrored in the appearance of the town itself. In the later years of the eighteenth century and the opening years of the nineteenth, however, events were taking place in Newcastle which would prepare the way for the transformation of the town.

# 4 All things connect[1]

T he defeat of the Jacobite army of Charles Edward Stuart – 'Bonn Prince Charlie' – at Culloden in 1746 seems an unlikely starti point in the search for the seeds of Richard Grainger's transformati of Newcastle. However, this was one of a number of historical even including the great flood of 1771 and the turnpiking of roads to the Nor which fell like pebbles into the quiet waters of eighteenth-centu Newcastle. The consequent ripples connected and interacted to begin t change of the long undisturbed appearance of Newcastle town.

The disappearance of the threat of cross-border attack from the Sco with the defeat of the Jacobite rebellion was an important factor in t growth of the town beyond its medieval walls. Not only could it safe spread into areas which had previously only been attractive to less desirab elements, principally industry and the poor, but it was also able to begin t dismantling of the walls themselves. Initially the stretch along the Quay w removed in 1763 allowing the greater use of the quay itself and there increasing the importance of the streets which connected the quayside wi the upper parts of the town.[2] From 1795 to 1798 the Pandon, Close and Sa Gates were demolished and in 1811 the Postern and West Gates we

**Groined Archway of Newgate, Newcastle during the demolition of the Outer Gate, 1823. An engraving by W. Pybus from a drawing by T.M. Richardson Snr**

The opening out of transport routes, of access routes to the river and of plots of developable land created by the removal of parts of the Town Wall and its Gates was fundamental to the expansion of the town in the late eighteenth and early nineteenth centuries.

Laing Art Gallery

The Tyne Bridge in
1772 after the flood

Newcastle's medieval
bridge had stood since
1250 and had been last
repaired on the advice of
John Smeaton in 1770.
However, a raging torrent
of water, reaching to the
tops of the bridge's arch-
es, swept it away on the
night of Saturday 17th
November 1771. Carried
away with it were not
only the shops and hous-
es which lined the struc-
ture but also a significant
link with the town's past.

removed allowing the further development of the town's streets. Indeed the removal of the town wall from Newgate to Pilgrim Street was to play an important part in the redevelopment of the town and the careers of various men, including Richard Grainger.

This opening out of the town which began with the removal of parts of its defensive walls took place at a time when, partly as a result of the experience of the Jacobite rising, but also to meet the need to move the products of early industries, the value of improved transport and communication links was being recognised. By 1764 the journey time from London to York had been halved from four days to two by the improvement in construction and maintenance of roads.[3] The first turnpike road from Durham to Newcastle was authorised in 1747 and the need to bring the standard of the town's roads to the same level was accepted, even by the Corporation.

The great flood of 1771 which brought the destruction of the medieval Tyne Bridge was similarly a watershed in the history of the development of the town. The removal of the twelfth century bridge, physically and symbolically swept away Newcastle's medieval transport links with the rest of England. In its place rose a sturdy stone bridge with fine masonry and elegant balustrades,[4] which, despite the practical problems caused by its narrowness and the still convoluted routes leading from it, made a statement about the directions both the road and the town were taking.

Until the late eighteenth century building within the core of the town had been spasmodic and piecemeal, but it had nevertheless presented a noble picture in its medieval heyday. In 1609 it was described as the "glory of all

**The Tyne Bridge c.1848**

The elegance of the eighteenth century bridge constructed after the loss of its predecessor in 1771 and the grandeur of the Moot Hall were centrepieces of the improving town in the opening decades of the nineteenth century. As the pace of change grew ever more rapid, by the time of this view in the late 1840s the value to the town of both structures was under question.

the towns in this country"[5] and in 1633 "beyond all compare the fairest a richest town in England, inferior for wealth and building to no city sa London and Bristol."[6] Celia Fiennes, visiting Newcastle in 1698, describ it as "a noble town … it most resembles London of any place in England, buildings lofty and large …"[7] However it was, like all towns of the tim fragile.[8] Buildings were continually destroyed by fire. The populatio regularly denuded by the severity of the justice system (twenty-two peop were executed on the Town Moor on a single day in 1650 – fifteen for bei witches) and more importantly by plague, most notably in 1636 when t staggering number of 5,037 people are said to have died from it and in 16 when a further 924 citizens were carried off by a plague, bizarrely named t "jolly rant".

Daniel Defoe in the 1720s was still able to describe Newcastle spacious but by the middle of the eighteenth century some infilling had tak place within the medieval street pattern of the town, particularly in t formation of yards such as Old George Yard. At the same time, howev new desirable streets were being constructed, notably Clavering Place a Hanover Square, as part of a fundamental change in the residential pattern the town. The Close, for example, had been the home of merchan burgesses and members of the aristocracy since at least the fifteenth centu but by the early eighteenth century it had begun to decline. In 1736 t

ed's Plan of
vcastle 1610

vcastle was
cribed in 1609 as
e glory of all the
ns in this country", it
nevertheless small,
wded and plague-
len. Speed's map
phasises its compact
ire and the role and
oortance of the town
ls.

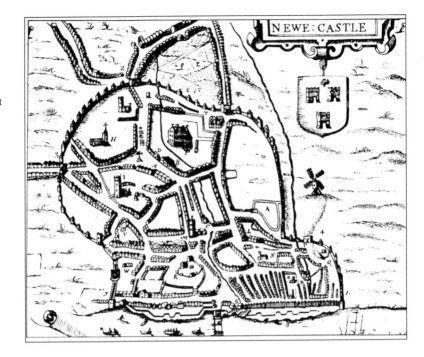

Plan of Newcastle,
graved for the
verend Henry
urne 1736 (after
nes Corbridge 1725)

hing out beyond its
dieval boundaries the
out of the town
gan to reflect social
anges within the
lls, whilst new
ldings, roperies and
hards illustrate the
ly expansion beyond
m. The continuing
portance of the river
de is shown by the
ead of housing
stward almost to the
uth of the Ouseburn.

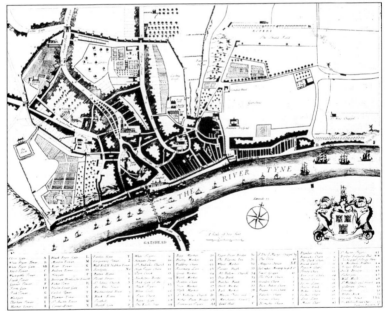

historian Henry Bourne observed that "Of late Years these Houses have been forsaken, and their wealthier Inhabitants have chosen the higher Parts of the Town."[9] The chares of the Quayside similarly slipped into squalor as the urban aristocracy moved away. This movement of the disaffected wealthy and the influential in time spread to the areas beyond the immediate riverside, and by 1800 Pilgrim Street, once a favoured area of the opulent,

23

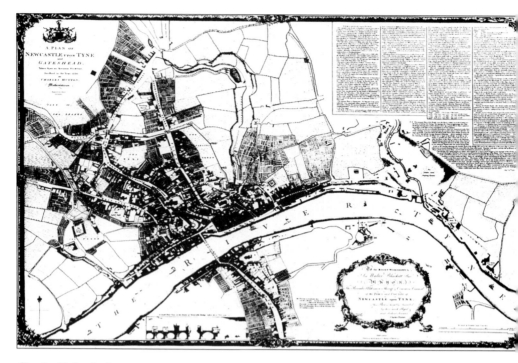

**Charles Hutton's plan of Newcastle 1772**

Newcastle by 1770 stood ready for sweeping change, spreading along the river edge, beyond the walls, into the Forth, expanding and developing without order or control.

began to fall into decay. With opportunities opened up to build beyond walls, elegant streets of houses such as Saville Row, started in the 177 Ellison Place, Brandling Place and Charlotte Square were built to house migrating 'middle classes'.

The improvements in the streets and the development of gen residential parts of the town were accompanied by a heightened regard architecturally fine public buildings. Thus the last three decades of eighteenth century saw the erection of a number of impressive buildi which grace the city to this day – All Saints Church, the remode Guildhall, the elegant Assembly Rooms. When, at the end of the first dec of the new century William Stokoe designed the new Moot Hall in the Ca Garth on severe classical lines employing polished stone, the use of materials and architectural style with which Richard Grainger would fo his streets were established in the town.[10]

The removal of the gates and walls also allowed the construction of a improvements to communicating roads as well as new residential a commercial streets. The development of the New Street along the north Sandgate in 1776 (in time to become City Road) probably owed more to importance of the glass industry based at the mouth of the Ouseburn, increasing industrial use of the North Shore and the historic links with No Shields and its salt industry rather than any desire to improve the to However, the construction in 1783 of Mosley Street, which had be promoted by Alderman Mosley and Nathaniel Clayton and designed by Corporation architect David Stephenson, and Dean Street in 1787 mar the first major and planned alteration to the street pattern of the town. The broad and paved Dean Street was designed to improve the access between the lower and upper parts of the town and to connect with the newly constructed Mosley Street. Mosley Street quickly became the fashionable commercial heart of the town; new and prestigious buildings sprang up along its length – the Post Office, banks, shops – all completing a street which reflected the rising economic prosperity of the town.[11] The building of Collingwood Street in 1809-10 extended this complex of main streets and formed an important communication link with Westgate Street, creating a road from east to west which still forms the principal cross-town route today.

Within the town, however, there was a growing dichotomy between the old streets where surviving long, narrow medieval burgage plots extended back from the street frontage, and the newer streets where the less elongated rectangular building plots provided far more convenient sites for the construction of new commercial and residential buildings.[12] The division into tenements of the houses of the fleeing urban gentry further drove down the social standing of the older parts of the town. A letter in the *Gentleman's Magazine* of January 1807 gave expression to this state of affairs: "Alas! how mortified we were to find it just as it was said to be a hundred years ago. The streets are paved with little round cobblestones, so full of deep holes as to be dangerous to ride along, for they have not been repaired for the last century ... Yet they boast of their Corporation having above thirty thousand pounds a year. There is an old joke against canny Edinburgh that they used formerly to empty certain containing vessels into the streets from upper storeys, but at Newcastle they now, very coolly lay them down at noon-day and the Scavenger, perhaps, comes and takes them up again next week, to the no small annoyance of passengers ... The street called 'The Side' would be a disgrace to any Corporation in England."[13] Newcastle, however, was a town of contrast, and whilst the ancient streets stagnated, new development opportunities sprang up all around.

**The Side in 1827. An engraving by W. Collard from a drawing by T.M. Richardson Snr**

Tall timber-framed medieval houses still dominated large parts of Newcastle even as the new streets and houses began to take form in the higher parts of the town. The contrast was sharp. "The street called 'The Side' would be a disgrace to any Corporation in England" observed one visitor.

# 5  A Vast Quantity of Ground

B y the beginning of the nineteenth century Newcastle was experiencing what would now be called a property boom. Ships, which a hundred years earlier had arrived for the coal trade empty but for ballast, now arrived with cargoes for the growing town. When the trade embargoes of the Napoleonic Wars were lifted and the maritime threat to the country had been expunged at Trafalgar in 1805, ships full of Baltic timber, Quebec Pine, Norway timber, Honduras Mahogany, American timber, cedar wood, slates from Scotland and elsewhere, Roman cement and all manner of building materials arrived in the Tyne. Brick and tile works proliferated – at St Anthony's, Shield Field, Blaydon Burn and other locations. Raffyards storing timber were established along the river's edge where the tidal flow helped to preserve the wood. Newspapers, meanwhile, were awash with advertisements for the sale or lease of building plots – landowners were cashing in on a changing economic climate in which agents, architects, developers and builders took a grip upon the development of the town. The land of men like Thomas Burdon was being offered in Jesmond as sites for housing or as in the case of a field in Pandon, for the making of bricks. The role of the agent/architect was personified by the spiralling influence of John Dobson, through whom many of these opportunities presented themselves via the local newspapers:

2nd February 1811 – "To be sold – a variety of sites of Freehold Ground, the Property of Thomas Burdon Esq ... A plan of the whole may be seen at the house of Mr Dobson at Chirton."[1]

2nd March 1811 – "To be sold – several Freehold Sites for building at the Barras Bridge ... apply Mr John Dobson, architect."[2]

1st April 1813 – "Freehold Building Ground to the east and west sides of Pandon Dean ... apply Mr Dobson."[3]

16th March 1813 – "Various building sites for dwelling houses and manufactories in two new streets about to be opened adjoining Forth Banks and Forth Lane ... apply Mr Dobson."[4]

18th May 1814 – "Four Freehold fields in the Township of Jesmond adjoining the new buildings there lately erected by Thomas Burdon ... apply Mr Dobson."[5]

1st April 1815 – "Freehold Building Sites – in continuation of Ellison Plac[e] … apply Mr Dobson."[6]

29th March 1817 – "A quantity of freehold ground to be sold in the mos[t] eligible and airy part of Percy Street where it is projected to build a crescen[t] … apply Mr Dobson."[7]

However, one piece of land which was not put on the market was the prim[e] development opportunity of its day. Whilst residential property grew aroun[d] the old confines and the commercial centre of the town moved into th[e] Mosley Street-Collingwood Street area, the continued spread an[d] development of the town northwards was hindered by what was, at the time[,] the most remarkable of the surviving medieval aspects of the town – th[e] extensive private estate of Anderson Place and the neighbouring Nun['s] Fields. Covering twelve acres and dominating the northern part of the tow[n] within the walls, the grounds originally formed part of the nunnery of S[t] Bartholomew. On dissolution the nunnery passed into private hands and th[e] house which had become "so great a receptacle of Scots" and other deeme[d] ne'er-do-wells, was pulled down to be replaced in 1580 by a noble mansio[n]

**John Dobson (1787-1865) as a young man, from a painting by John Dixon**

The rise of professional men to significance in the late eighteenth century was nowhere better illustrated than in the role of the architect/surveyor. Following in the footsteps of David Stephenson, the architect of many of the town's earlier improvements, John Dobson was by the late 1820s at the forefront of his profession – a position he maintained until his death almost four decades later.

Laing Art Gallery

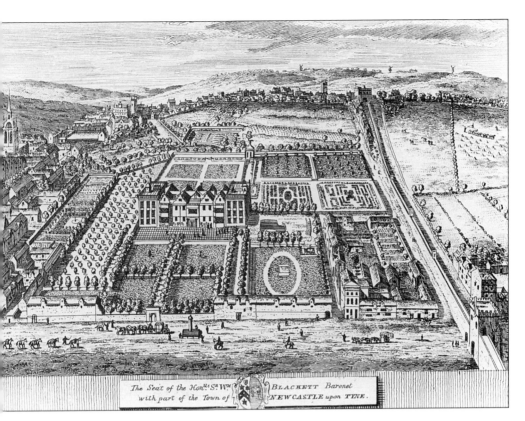

The Seat of the Hon.ᵇˡᵉ Sʳ Wᵐ BLACKETT Baronet
with part of the Town of NEWCASTLE upon TYNE.

## The Anderson Estate, 1702

The location and significance of the Anderson estate can be readily understood from the eighteenth century plans of Newcastle. The size of the estate in itself and in relation to the rest of the town, particularly in conjunction with the adjacent Nuns Fields, is captured in this view looking across Pilgrim Street. In 1702 it was the seat of Sir William Blackett; by the early nineteenth century it was a medieval anachronism at the heart of the town.

constructed by Robert Anderson, a wealthy merchant. On Speed's map of the town of 1610 (see page 23) it is referred to as the "Newe House", and is described by the Newcastle writer, Grey, in the same period as a "princely mansion"[8] – good enough to be used to house King Charles I in captivity for ten months following his surrender to the Scots in 1646. Robert Anderson also purchased the grounds, filled up the dene which intersected the land, and converted it into a pleasant field. The house and lands, in time, were sold to the Blackett family who added two large wings to the property. In 1736 Bourne described it as "no less than very stately and magnificent, being supposed the most of any house in the whole kingdom within a walled town. It is surrounded by a vast quantity of ground; that part of it which faces the street is thrown into walks and grass plots, beautified with images and beset with trees … The other part of the ground on the west side of it is all a garden, exceedingly neat and curious, adorned with many and the most beautiful statues and other curiosities."[9]

The value of the land in the future development of the town was recognised by the Corporation in the period when they turned their thoughts to improvement. The Corporation apparently considered its purchase when Sir Walter Blackett died in 1777 but were hamstrung by expenditure on the new bridge and the developing proposals for Mosley Street and Dean Street.[10] Instead it was purchased by George Anderson, a prosperous builder,

**Anderson Place, 1825.
etched by W.W. Pybus
from a drawing by T.M.
Richardson Snr**

The house had its origins
in the the late sixteenth
century but the name was
not adopted until the
early nineteenth. It was
constructed by Robert
Anderson in 1580, Sir
William Blackett added
two incongruous wings
to it following his
purchase of the property
in 1675 and in 1782 his
descendant Sir Thomas
Blackett sold the house
to a successful builder
Mr George Anderson,
whose son, Major
Anderson named it
Anderson Place. Major
Anderson's occupancy of
the mansion was to be
the last.

who, it is thought, converted it into three dwellings. The property passed c
his death to his son Major Anderson who renamed it "Anderson Place".

When, on 7th January 1826, an advertisement appeared in the *Newcast*
*Courant* offering "To be let, the Nun's Field. Major Anderson has bee
induced to divide the said Field into Sites for the above purpose. Particula
apply to Mr Dobson, architect,"[11] the thoughts of some must have turned
the opportunity for redevelopment on a major scale. The stage was bein
prepared for Richard Grainger, who had risen in the 1820s to a position a
the town's prominent builder, to transform the centre of Newcastle.

# 6 A Raw Lad Like Grainger

Over a period of twenty years Richard Grainger rose from a joiner's apprentice to be the leading and most influential builder and property developer in the North East of England. In 1833 at the age of thirty-six, even before he began his greatest work – the wholesale redevelopment of the town centre – he was awarded a silver tureen and salver at a public dinner in his honour to mark his achievements in the town. His career even to this point had been, by any standards, meteoric.

Richard Grainger was a son of Newcastle. He was born on the 9th October 1797 in High Friar Lane, a street squeezed between the Nun's Field and the Town Wall, which led from High Friar Chare, broadly on the line of the present Blackett Street. In time Grainger would almost single-handedly transform the whole area surrounding the site of his birthplace. At the time of his birth, however, High Friar Chare was described as having "a long, dead brick wall on one side, and the town wall mouldering into ruins on the other…"[1] The Grainger family are said to have occupied two tenement rooms in an upstairs level, but a note accompanying a sketch of his birthplace suggests that Richard's parents occupied a room on the ground floor. Richard is claimed by some to have been the second of two sons born to Thomas and Amelia Grainger. The St Andrew's Church baptism register, however, records him as their fourth son. Other documents also record the existence of four brothers, George, probably the eldest, William of which little is known other than that he died in Thirsk in 1823, John, born on 17th July 1791 and Richard himself. A daughter, Amelia, was born in 1794. His father, Thomas, was a native of the County of Cumberland, the family possibly originating from the Grainger family of Brough,[2] although the St Andrew's Baptism register records the family name as Grange.[3] Thomas was a day labourer, later to be described by the *Monthly Chronicle* as a "porter pokeman gannin' on the quay". Richard's mother, Amelia, was the daughter of Thomas Burt, (or Brunt in the St Andrew's baptism register) a private soldier, serving in Gibraltar, where Amelia was born in 1755. When Thomas Grainger died about the year 1809 or 1810 Amelia, described as "an excellent woman, honest, frugal, industrious, clever and neat-handed," continued to support the family by stocking-grafting, glove-making and clear starching.[4] By this time however, Richard's elder brother George was already an apprentice bricklayer and Richard was reaching the end of his school years and was himself taking his first steps in the building trade.

**Richard Grainger's birthplace in High Friar Lane (c.1830), from *Sketches Illustrative of the life of Richard Grainger* by John Green, 1843**

Exemplifying the huge contrast between his origins and his achievements, small, aged and hemmed in by medieval walls and narrow dirty streets, his birthplace was typical of the properties which gave way to the new grander designs. John Green's appended note to his illustration marks the ground floor rooms to the left of the sketch as those of the Grainger family.

Richard Grainger's school years were spent at St Andrew's Parish Charity School. The school had been set up in Newgate Street by Sir William Blackett in the early years of the eighteenth century. By the time the young Richard Grainger attended the school it had moved to premises in Percy Street, where reading, writing and accounts were taught. Each year the children were supplied with a "green coat and cap, a waistcoat, a pair of leather breeches, two shirts and bands, and three pairs of shoes and stockings."[5] On leaving the school, generally at the age of fourteen, pupils were given a Bible, a Prayer Book, Mr Lewis' Catechism and *The Whole Duty of Man* and 40 shillings "to put them out Apprentice or Equip them for Services."

Richard Grainger's 40 shillings must have been put to good use. He became an apprentice with a master carpenter, John Brown, under whose tutelage he learned the rudiments of the building trade. In about 1816 he thought to have set up business, in a small way, with his eldest brother George carrying out building work, their first substantial job being the reconstruction of their next-door neighbour's house in High Friar Lane. Possibly even while this work was in progress George became ill and died, leaving Richard to carry on the business alone. John Green, in his *Sketches Illustrative of the Life of Richard Grainger*, identifies numbers 3, 4, 5, and 6 Strawberry Place as the first houses built by Richard Grainger "on his own account". His work came to the attention of a number of influential men who it is thought Grainger had met through a growing interest in the Methodist movement. Certainly the work ethics inherent in Methodism at this time were imbued in the young builder. He is said to have worked daily from 3 a.m. to 9 p.m. to guarantee the success of his first major contract – the construction, in 1819, of a number of

"particularly delightful small Georgian houses,"[6] to form a new street – Higham Place – for Alderman Batson in the increasingly desirable area beyond the old town walls.

The pioneering female journalist Harriet Martineau, whom we will meet on several occasions describing Grainger's works and career, reported how scorn was initially poured on the idea that the building of Higham Place could be entrusted to "a raw lad like Grainger". However, the success of Grainger's first large undertaking was the springboard for a series of contracts to build houses in the new middle-class residential areas of the town. The erection of two houses in Percy Street and larger numbers in New Bridge Street and Carliol Street marked him as a growing figure within the booming trade. His marriage to Rachel Arundale, the eldest daughter of Joseph Arundale a wealthy businessman in one of Tyneside's other burgeoning industries, the tanning and leather trade, on 7th October 1821

reflected the social position he had already achieved. Rachel, whom it is sa
Grainger first met at "class meetings", also brought to the marriage a dow
of £5,000 which allowed Grainger to extend his interests, his business, h
connections and his position amongst the group of men who were at th
centre of the growth and redevelopment of Newcastle.

As the appearance and identity of the tow
changed, the role of the surveyor and archite
became pivotal. At this time, John Dobson an
Thomas Oliver were, perhaps, the most influenti
of this small group of professional men. Dobso
had set up an office in Pilgrim Street in 181
before moving to Mosley Street in 1815. Olive
who had worked under Dobson for six year
started his own practice in 1821. The removal
the stretch of Town Wall along the northe
boundary of the medieval town in 1823 allowe
Dobson and Oliver to plan, propose and brin
about the replacement of what had been a dirt
unpaved, "almost unpassable street", a "useless waste, where manure wa
deposited" with a new broad street – Blackett Street "considered a grar
affair … from its width and regularity."[7] The growing reputation, standir
and wealth of Grainger saw him by 1824 involved in the schem
constructing thirty-one brick built houses to Thomas Oliver's design on th
north side of the new street.

An important factor in Grainger's rise was his relationship with ke
personnel. He is thought to have been assisted in these enterprises by h
friend and attorney John Fenwick, just as his earliest ventures had bee
carried out under the wing of his Methodist mentor William Batson and h
later ones were undertaken with the support of John Clayton.[8] The origin
his contacts with John Fenwick, as with Alderman Batson, appear to lie
his connections with the Methodist movement, although his interest appea
to be one of business rather than religion, for he was married and indeed h
many children were baptised in St Andrew's Parish Church. However, th
contacts he had made with people of this class and particularly with men
influence such as Dobson were critical factors in Grainger's progressio
from a run of the mill, if relatively prosperous, builder to the deliverer of th
foremost architecturally designed and planned developments of the day.
the ten years following his work in Blackett Street, Grainger completed th
three most prestigious developments which had to that date been undertake
in the town – Eldon Square, Leazes Terrace and the Royal Arcade. With the
construction Newcastle would begin to foster an air of elegance befitting i
position as a hugely important commercial centre and regional capital.

# 7   "The Pride of the Town"

Eldon Square c.1841.
Collard after T.M.
Richardson Snr

Eldon Square was
immediately
acknowledged as the
town's most graceful
development. It was
unprecedented in
Newcastle for its size,
uniformity and building
quality. Ranges were
faced in fine ashlar
masonry and added to
the prestige of the
buildings in a town
where the residential
architecture was
overwhelmingly of brick.

It was a logical progression of Grainger's career, having completed his work on Blackett Street, to undertake the construction of Eldon Square. The Square had been proposed as part of the laying out of Blackett Street. Occupying the site of the envisaged square was a garden of old barren fruit trees. The Corporation bought the site and asked Thomas Oliver to prepare a plan and model illustrating his development proposals. These were presented to the Common Council who sought the opinion of Dobson, who, according to Oliver, "afterwards furnished a plan containing several alterations."[1] Work began in 1825-26, with Grainger building all but four of the houses in the three-sided square.

The houses were ranged around an ornamental shrubbery, each range containing ten houses designed by Dobson, built in the fashionable Palladian style with polished stone fronts and first floor cast-iron balconies. The historian McKenzie observed in 1827 that "this square will be one of the proudest monuments of the taste and spirit of the Corporation in modern times."[2] Grainger was at the same time also engaged in the construction of what became the Northern Academy of Fine Arts on the other side of

**Eldon Square c.1841. An engraving by Collard after T.M. Richardson Snr**

"The three great blocks of the square, the east and west of 27 bays, the north of 39 bays, were each symmetrical, their angles accented with Doric pilasters, and on the centre block there was to be a portico of six Ionic columns, but this was not built. The first floor, with very tall windows, a *piano nobile* in the Palladian tradition, had cast iron balconies with Greek honeysuckle decoration." (*The Tyneside Classical Tradition*, Tyne and Wear County Council, Museums, 1980)

Laing Art Gallery

Blackett Street, a building described by Thomas Oliver as "solely appropriated for the public Exhibition of Pictures and for the purposes of a Diorama. The interior of the building is formed into two octagonal apartments, by columns that can be removed at pleasure."[3] Grainger may also have been busy with the formation of St Mary's Place to the design of John Dobson. This project was finished in 1830 – at least a year before the prolonged work on Eldon Square came to a successful conclusion. By which time Grainger was engaged in not only building the town's most prestigious developments but also purchasing more property on which to construct his own increasingly grandiose schemes.

On 7th of March 1829, the first stones were laid in the construction of Leazes Terrace and Leazes Crescent. This must have been a highly public event, as an estimated twenty thousand people passed nearby as they headed for the Town Moor where Jane Jameson – "a most disgusting and abandoned female." – was that day hung for stabbing her mother to death with a red hot poker.[4] The stark contrast between the continuing barbarity and popularity of public executions and the genteel connotations of the design and appearance of Leazes Terrace is just one example of the divisions inherent in the growing town. The scale of Grainger's Leazes proposal was greeted with alarm by his solicitor John Fenwick who advised him to "retire upon the £20,000 he had now realised, instead of risking all in so vast an enterprise."[5] Grainger's scheme was to erect on the "high, open and airy" Leazes, described as "a wide grazing ground to the north of the town, adjoining the moor,"[6] a block of seventy lofty houses, designed by Thomas Oliver, in the form of an elongated square in a classical style with small gardens to the

Leazes Terrace c.1841.
Collard after J.W.
Carmichael

Leazes Terrace – the
pride of the Town – was
Grainger's finest
monument to elegant
living. It was designed
not only to live in but
also to promenade
round. The zenith of his
work as a builder of
residential developments,
following its completion
Grainger turned his
attention to exploiting the
opportunities provided by
commercial building in
the town centre.

front and a paved terrace walk around the outside. The work which took five
years to complete also included the construction of "comfortable brick and
stucco two-storey cottages forming Leazes Crescent and Leazes Place." The
journalist Harriet Martineau referred to Leazes Terrace as "deservedly the
pride of the town."[7]

Grainger's third great work of this period was the Royal Arcade, erected
at the eastern end of Mosley Street, a site now occupied by part of the
Pilgrim Street roundabout complex. Although first envisaged as a solution to
the town's pressing need for a new Corn Exchange, the structure became the
town's first indoor retail and commercial centre. Its origins lay in a perverse
and protracted debate regarding opposing bids for the site of a new covered
Corn Exchange which exercised the minds of the Common Council for many
sessions. Letters were written to the newspapers regarding the merits of
alternative sites and a committee was set up to consider the issue. Grainger
was keen to pursue the building of the new corn market on the land he had
purchased at the end of Mosley Street but the Council committee opted for
a rival site in Middle Street The issue was not finally resolved until many
years later and the building which Grainger constructed in the course of less
than a year, probably once again to the design of either Dobson or Oliver,
was to serve a different purpose. As a commercial and shopping centre its
noble and elegant appearance, both internally and externally, gave the arcade
many advantages over the still predominantly unpaved and medieval streets,,
but its position on the fringe of the town centre worked against its success.
The location as the site for a Corn Exchange would have had many plus-
points but the limited access – the rear of the building led out on to the

**The Interior of the Royal Arcade, c.1841. Collard after John Dobson**

The Royal Arcade was built as two office blocks, one facing Pilgrim Street and the other Manor Chare. Connecting the two was a narrow block forming the arcade itself. The inside was planned in the style of a modern shopping centre wherein pedestrians could walk past a number of different establishments and 'window shop'. Whilst the Pilgrim Street frontage and entrance with its prestigious banking premises met these ambitions, the long stairs, plainer elevation and less salubrious environs of Manor Chare undermined its popularity with its well-to-do clientele.

comparatively sordid, narrow confines of Manor Chare – was not ideal for the shopping and commercial arcade which was built. Nevertheless, it was an important addition to the town; into it moved the Post Office, the Stamp Excise and Permit Offices, the Savings Bank, The North of England Joint Stock Bank, many lawyers', engineers', and architects' offices, auction rooms, shops and steam and vapour bath rooms. The handsome stone front occupied by two banks, extended for 94 feet and rose to a lofty 75 feet. The interior, 250 feet long, 20 feet wide and 35 feet high, was lit by eight conical glass domes. The development was built at a cost of £40,000, bringing the estimated value of the properties built by Grainger to this time to an estimated £200,000.[8]

Of these three great works only Grainger's development in the Leazes survives intact. Eldon Square was a casualty of late 1960s and early 1970

**Design for the Royal Arcade, Newcastle upon Tyne, 1831. John Dobson and J.W. Carmichael**

John Dobson's *Design for the Royal Arcade* expresses the severe grandeur of the frontage and the entrance way but it also portrays its overbearing size. Despite the milling crowd, there is a feeling of the isolation of the building which would mark it as Grainger's least successful commercial venture. Its situation on the periphery of the town centre was further exaggerated by Grainger's own town centre developments. It was nevertheless a massive and impressive addition to the town.

Laing Art Gallery

redevelopment, two sides of the Square being removed to make way for the then new Eldon Square Shopping Centre. The Royal Arcade, perhaps the least successful of all his works, was already in decline by 1860 when the Post Office moved out, and was considered for demolition in the 1880s. Its fate was finally sealed in 1963. Soon after, elements of the interior were, to the derision of many, reconstructed within the new office complex which replaced it on the same site, and Grainger's stone work dumped unceremoniously in spare ground at the City Stadium site in Warwick Street.[9] Despite being feted by the Corporation, local MPs and dignitaries for his achievement in building the Royal Arcade, the lessons to be learned from the bitter public wrangling over the Corn Exchange and the decision by the Council committee against his proposal were not lost on a man who had become Newcastle's foremost builder and developer. In preparing his next, largest and boldest plan – nothing short of the wholesale redevelopment of the centre of the town – he was careful to ensure the confidentially of the scheme for as long as possible and to secure the backing of the Council.

# 8    Mr Grainger Acts

hether, as some Victorian commentators suggested, Richa[r]
Grainger recognised the need for a new town centre even as [a]
raw apprentice or whether he, as more contemporary historia[n]
have suggested, had shown no interest whatsoever in the redevelopment [of]
the streets prior to the 1830s is open to debate. The image of the young m[an]
looking, perhaps even from his own home, at the underused and decayi[ng]
grounds of Anderson Place and the Nun's Fields and envisaging t[he]
Metropolis he was to build, was attractive to those who sought to lioni[se]
him. This was particularly true of the eulogies which followed his death a[nd]
in the writings of the journalist Harriet Martineau, who visited the town [in]
1840 when Grainger's greatest works had just been completed. However, [in]
reality, the need to improve the upper part of the town, particularly throu[gh]
the exploitation of the Anderson owned lands was recognised by others als[o.]
The architects, John Dobson and Thomas Oliver both published propos[als]
for a new layout of streets some years before Richard Grainger placed h[is]
historic proposals before Newcastle's Common Council on 22nd May 183[4.]

John Dobson's plan, produced in 1824 and published in 1827, propos[ed]
to establish a new civic palace or Mansion House on the site of Anders[on]
Place, utilising the existing estate roads to form a grand tree-lined approac[h,]
to construct a large market on the Nuns Fields and to create an extension [to]
Blackett Street which would enhance its role as a principal thoroughfar[e.]
Oliver's plan, presented to the Corporation in 1830, concentrated [on]
improving the main communication routes of the town.[1] Both architec[ts]
placed an emphasis on the Blackett Street area where, no doubt, their rece[nt]
building activity would come to the fore. Oliver also proposed a number [of]
new streets, notably one which would link the prestigious houses he h[ad]
designed for Grainger in the Leazes with the town centre. The plan whi[ch]
Grainger produced shared the general approach of supplying wi[de]
thoroughfares and improving access but also proposed a thoroughly origin[al]
concept – the development of a completely new commercially based tow[n]
centre.

Following the death of Major Anderson in 1831, Grainger must hav[e]
realised that there was potential for such proposals to become reality – t[he]
Reverend Dibdin observing that "While others think, Mr Grainger acts."[2] [He]
probably drew up his proposals in 1833 but on consulting John Clayton, t[he]
Town Clerk, was persuaded to wait for a year before presenting them to th[e]

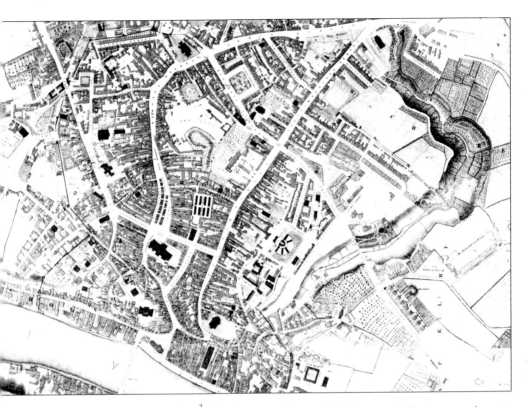

Corporation.[3] That he was willing to do this suggests that no one else was similarly placed to undertake such a wide-ranging scheme and that the wrangle over the Corn Market would not be repeated with this, his greatest project. Grainger's plan had at its core the acquisition, demolition and redevelopment of Anderson Place, the Nuns Fields and a swathe of land, occupied by numerous old dwellings, extending principally southward to Mosley Street; he proposed to fashion a new street pattern, based on three main thoroughfares with adjoining and linking streets. The new focal point of the town would be a 'circus' at the point where two of his new broad streets met the already improved area of Eldon Square and Blackett Street, to be called Seven Dials Circus (more familiar to us now as the Monument). The principal street, in time to be called Grey Street but originally envisaged as Upper or New Dean Street, was to sweep through the old estate grounds, down the re-contoured line of the Lort Burn, which still divided and encumbered the town, to meet Dean Street at its junction with Mosley Street. In so doing, Grainger thereby connected his new development with the already improved axis of late eighteenth century streets, which themselves had been added to by the construction of Collingwood Street in the first decade of the nineteenth century. This made the new street the main through route of the town. Also by linking the modern streets to the south of the town with the newly improved and highly prestigious area he had helped to create to the north, Grainger ensured that the streets he was about to create would

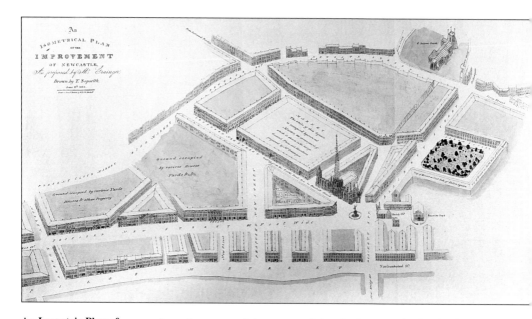

## An Isometric Plan of the Improvement of Newcastle as proposed by Mr Grainger June 11th 1834

Grainger's proposals for a new town centre were sweeping – the plan produced and presented to the Town Council to illustrate his new streets expressed the scale of the scheme, but the isometric view, produced for public display by Thomas Sopwith and shaded in appropriate colours to show the stone buildings and slate roofs demonstrated the quality as well as the breadth of the vision.

Laing Art Gallery

form the centre of the town and thereby become the focal point and the mos important part of Newcastle.

From the Seven Dials Circus a second major new street, Grainger Stree would link the new town centre directly with the top of the Bigg and Groa Market area and also allow the later development of a connection with th proposed Neville Street, the residential areas of Westgate and the routes t the west. The third principal street, Clayton Street, would run from Blacke Street and Eldon Square to Newgate Street, opening up the potential of connection to Westgate Street and to Percy Street and from there to the mai road north. A series of side streets, to become Hood Street, (named afte John Lionel Hood, Mayor of Newcastle in 1834-35) Nun Street, Shakespear Street and Nelson Street would link the new thoroughfares together and als connect the new streets with the ancient path of Pilgrim Street. Market Stree would provide access to the proposed new market. Standing in the way o Grainger's grand design were the Butcher Market, built in 1808 betwee High Bridge and Mosley Street, and the Theatre Royal built by Davi Stephenson in 1788 at the head of Mosley Street. Both of which were, by th standards of the day, relatively new and both of which were on the line of th intended New Dean Street. Grainger's solution to these impediments was t once again, acquire and demolish the buildings and redevelop the land whils at the same time providing the town with prestigious replacements. The ne market was to be built on the former Nuns Field, with access from Grainge Street, Clayton Street, Nun Street, Nelson Street and the new Market Stree The new theatre was to stand at a most prominent point on the new mai street, though the original intention was to construct it on an adjacent spot o the opposite side of the street.

Of the new streets Grey Street, as it would be eventually called, was t be 80 feet wide with a twelve feet wide flagged path on either side. Th

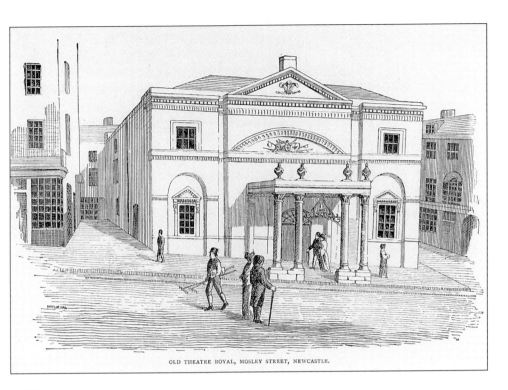

OLD THEATRE ROYAL, MOSLEY STREET, NEWCASTLE.

**e old Theatre Royal,
osley Street, 1827**

vid Stephenson's
eatre Royal was
scribed by the histori-
Charleton as "unsur-
ssed by any provincial
eatre in the country." It
as removed to make
y for Grainger's new
velopments.

ainger's willingness to
molish the relatively
dern and aesthetically
mired Theatre, togeth-
with the still newer
tcher Market, reflects
s ambition and the
eeping nature of the
oposals.

surface of the road was to be macadamised, as were Grainger Street and Clayton Street which were to be 70 feet wide. The streets were to be lined with offices and shops with dwelling houses or warehouses above, and with major public buildings, most notably the spacious two acres of covered market. All the buildings were to be fronted in polished stone "chastely ornamented", and built in ranges to elegant neo-classical designs. Provision was also to be made for the supply of gas lighting and water and for the construction of sewers. The plan was ambitious, sweeping and breathtaking. Grainger had assiduously fostered the support of John Clayton, partly as a result of which, the Common Council was quick to request that the proposal and plans should be presented to an early meeting of the Council and that they should also be displayed to the people of the town for their reaction. The need for improvement, previous lost opportunities, the lack of need for excessive public expenditure and the memory of the recent horrors of the cholera outbreak of 1832 all added to the Council's willingness to view the proposal in a favourable light.

The Common Council agreed that a special meeting be held on 12th June 1834 at 11.00 a.m. in the Mayor's Chamber to consider the proposal. They requested that a lithographed plan and an accompanying explanation be circulated to members of the Council and be publicly exhibited. On the 29th May the plans were displayed in Mr Small's Auction Rooms in Grainger's own Royal Arcade and caused considerable excitement. Voices were raised against the scheme by landlords fearing declining property

**Demolition of Houses in Pilgrim Street, 1835**

Considerable demolition of older properties was required to make way for the new streets. Pilgrim Street marked the eastern boundary of the new town centre. Partly improved by fine new adjoining streets and partly the victim of decline and decay it lost the importance it once had as a main thoroughfare. This situation continued until almost a century after Grainger's major changes, when the building of the New Tyne Bridge restored the fortunes of the street.

values in other parts of the town, from residents whose property was to engulfed by the development, by users of the threatened Butcher Market a by traders in the older streets foreseeing the movement of custom to the m comfortable and elegant confines of the new streets. Overall, though, t popular feeling was very much in favour of the changes, the *Newcas Journal*, a strong advocate for Grainger's scheme remarked that "The me of this case are so obvious."[4] Five thousand signatures were appended to publicly displayed plans, and petitions to the Council were overwhelmin, pro-Grainger. The meeting of the 12th June accepted the plans, Graing immediately concluded his negotiations for the purchase of Anderson Pla and on Tuesday, 15th July, the agreement between Grainger and t Corporation for the redevelopment of a major part of the town was seal "The bells of the churches in Newcastle rang several merry peals … same evening Mr Grainger's workmen were regaled with a plentiful sup of strong ale – which drew together a great crowd of spectators, who excited feelings led them to acts of violence. After being desired to dep they became furious and broke into the mansion called Anderson Place and destroyed the whole of a splendid staircase."[5] The redevelopment a transformation of Newcastle had, however informally, begun.

# The Extraordinary Magician

**9**

If Grainger's plan was breathtaking, the speed with which it was implemented was awe-inspiring. A mere fortnight after the signing of the agreement the local newspaper was able to report that "Mr Grainger commenced to take levels and lay out the intended new markets and streets in the Nuns Field."[1] However, it was not only the speed but also the scale of the operations which beggared belief. With the path of his main street designed to follow the deep incision of the Lort Burn, "hills had to be levelled and valleys filled up."[2] The lines of new streets were indicated by poles stuck in the ground; the lie of the land was so irregular that the top of some were below the bottom of others. Harriet Martineau reported that "throughout a wide area the excavations for the streets were to the depth of 17 feet, and for the basement storey of the houses 27 feet ... valleys had to be filled to the depth of 35 feet. Sometimes it was necessary to make a descent an ascent and sometimes the reverse. All this was exclusive of the trenches for foundations which were in some places 54 feet deep."[3] Soil was carried away from the site in carts at a cost of 2*d* per load, one carter alone is said to have been paid £1,040. Some 250,000 loads, estimated at 18 cubic feet a load, were moved. Mountains of material were retained – sand was used for mortar, whilst brick clay was retained for the on-the-spot production of bricks. The brickworks Grainger set up on the site augmented the supplies of Baltic timber brought into the river, the stone hewed from quarries at Elswick and Kenton and the materials he kept at his yards and workshops in Rankin's Court near Low Friar Street.[4] By the 4th October the whole foundations of the New Market were completed with one range of shops actually built, and the foundations of Grainger Street also complete. "Mr Grainger is one of the most extraordinary magicians that ever appeared" observed the writer William Howitt.[5]

Nothing was to stand in the way of progress. In preparing the plan Grainger had reached agreements regarding the old Butcher Market and the Theatre Royal. In the case of the former he had paid the Corporation £15,000 for the old market and agreed to sell the new market, on completion, back to the Corporation for £36,290. In the case of the Theatre Royal he agreed to pay £500 and furnish the proprietors with a new, larger and more prestigious theatre. Considering the quality and cost of the theatre they were to receive and the apparently unprofitable and failing nature of the old one this must have been viewed by the owners as a phenomenally attractive deal. It also

45

**The Butcher Market, c.1841. Collard after John Dobson**

"Entering by one of the archways from Grainger Street we pass through street after street of butchers' shops in which are displayed hecatombs of fresh killed meat. Rosy faced butchers surround us on all sides until we reach the regions where eggs, bacon and other provisions are displayed … in the centre a large stone basin with a fountain (nicknamed the Butcher's Spittoon), which on market days played and had a very pretty effect when the ducks brought for sale were allowed to swim in the water." (Charleton, 1888)

indicates the extent to which Grainger was willing to go to secure implementation of his scheme. Those who opposed the demolition of handsome Georgian Theatre building were undone by the speed Grainger's actions – he began the demolition of the roof within three ho of his purchase. A number of other properties were summarily dispatche the old Turks Head Inn, eight other public houses, eighty private houses a a large number of workshops and outbuildings. Such indecent ha characterised the scheme – not least because there was a considera amount of money involved in all of these works. The expenditure on la

preparation alone is thought to have amounted to £21,500 and the cost of wages and materials in the five years it took to complete the scheme was calculated at approximately half a million pounds.[6]

With his mighty workforce (Grainger was said to have been employing 2,000 men on the construction work) and a seemingly unstoppable momentum, the first buildings were complete by February 1835 and by October the massive new Grainger Market was ready for opening. The new Vegetable and Butcher Market was the largest and finest in the Kingdom, two acres in area, with fourteen entrances, 243 shops and two massive ornamental fountains, lit by gas-light, within a rectangle of stone-fronted classical terraces of shops and houses and covered with a complex timber roof structure. The celebrations which accompanied the opening of the market were elaborate; 2,000 people congregated in the market hall, with a further 300 ladies in a specially erected balcony, to witness an orgy of congratulations held within an atmosphere akin to Balshazaar's feast.

As the new streets grew, the glory of the buildings which were to line the wide paved thoroughfares became evident. In May 1836 the *Newcastle Chronicle* reported that the portion of the new street from High Bridge to Market Street and the New Turks Head frontage was nearing completion, that similar progress was being made on the other side of the new street and that on the site of the old Butcher Market – not a vestige of which remained – the foundations of another line of shops were being laid.[7] The foundations of the new Theatre Royal were begun in July 1836 and the building rose to its full majesty within six months with only the portico still to add. By December some of the shops on the street were occupied and by June of the

47

following year the street was complete other than "a site or two from whi the old buildings are not yet removed."[8] Both occupation of the ne properties and demolition of the old was being carried out as the schen advanced. The inconvenience of continual building work did not meet w everyone's approval, The Mayor at one point remarking that the blockage the streets was "outrageous and preposterous."[9] As the streets near completion, however, the *Newcastle Chronicle* provided long and detail descriptions of the progress of Mr Grainger's works in glowing term reporting the splendid advances being made on Grey Street, Grainger Stre Clayton Street and the rest. By June of the following year, 1838, the pap was able to print a list of all the occupiers of Grainger's streets and to rep that the last part of Grey Street where the old buildings still survived – t south-east corner junction with Mosley Street – was about to feel the wi of change – "the brick buildings will in a few weeks be pulled down and fine Corinthian termination to the street erected in a style corresponding wi the opposite corner."[10] Here, however, the development did not take place planned nor, indeed, even as reported in the newspaper. There were, in fa a number of pragmatic changes made by Grainger to his plan as the stree unfolded and the buildings rose.

The street plan as laid out by Grainger between 1834 and 1839 was he had initially proposed, with the exception of two small connecting stree leading from Grey Street, one to Pilgrim Street and one to High Bridg which were abandoned. In 1837 he proposed to expand his street patte firstly by the extension of Clayton Street to a junction with Westgate Stree which was carried out, and secondly by the extension of Grainger Stre from the Bigg Market south towards Neville Street, which was not.[11] Of t proposed buildings the contentious elements came to be sites in prestigio locations near the Circus at the very core of the development. On the site the northern terminus of Grainger Street the original isometric plan show a new church, a towering steepled Gothic edifice which was never bui Across the road at the important triangular plot formed by the heads Grainger Street and Grey Street the typical ranges of the original plan we subsumed within the construction of the splendid Central Exchan; Buildings. This building, a triumph of architectural design with its trip domes "crowned by an unlikely bunch of monstrous bronze feathers,"[12] w offered to the Corporation as, again, a Corn Exchange. The long standi dispute regarding the location of a new one was still not resolved but on again Grainger's proposal met with obstinacy from the interests within tl town and the Corporation. The building instead became a grand and opule all purpose meeting room, news room, coffee house and Central Exchang On the opening of the building, despite the rejection of the Corn Mark proposal, Grainger was once again feted at a public dinner. In a furth development, Grainger also petitioned unsuccessfully to construct a ne County Court, Town Court, Council Chamber and Judges' House in a pl

near the head of Grey Street to replace the Moot Hall and Guildhall which he offered to accept in exchange for this new facility.[13] The rejection of this proposal led him instead to build a banking headquarters for the Northumberland and Durham Bank, later to be used as Lloyd's Bank. Other more modest alterations were either offered or requested, Market Street was to be macadamised rather than paved and the Corporation requested the provision of a common 'privy' behind Nun Street.[14] Certainly not the most radical departure but perhaps the most tellingly significant alteration to the original plan, however, was the replacement of the proposed modest statue as the centre piece of the Seven Dials Circus with the impressive and commanding monument to Earl Grey.

The desire to erect a monument to mark the passing of the Great Reform Bill in 1832 and the part played in it by Charles, Earl Grey of Howick Hall Northumberland, was first voiced in North Shields. As early as June 1832 consideration was given to the siting of a monument in Northumberland Square, North Shields, and a design was drawn up by John Green, jun. architect, showing the great man atop a tall pillar.[15] The idea was seized on some years later in Newcastle where a meeting of subscribers considered three designs and models, the first by John Green of Blackett Street was chosen in preference to those submitted by John Dobson and Thomas Oliver. A special meeting of the Council on September 14th 1836 met to consider an application by the Grey Monument Committee for "leave to erect a monument near the head of Upper Dean Street and also to change the name of that street to Grey Street."[16] The proposal met some opposition – Mr J. Brandling wanted the monument placed on a high part of the Town Moor and others suggested alternative street names – Howick Street, Earl Grey Street and William Street (after the king, William IV) – but the plan was agreed and Grainger was asked "to convey to the Committee a sufficient space of ground at the head of Upper Dean Street and to change the name of that

**The Grey Column seen from Grey Street, c.1841. Collard after J.W. Carmichael.**

Unflatteringly described as "a landmark for benighted strangers who have lost their way in the toon" the heroically proportioned statue and lofty column has its tradition in the Statue to British Liberty erected at Gibside in 1757 and the near contemporary Nelson's Column in London (1839-41). Grainger's plan catered for a substantially less dominating centrepiece and the area now known (in a manner dismissive of the historic figure it commemorates) as "Monument" was conceived as the "Seven Dials Circus".

street to Grey Street."[17] The 134ft high Roman Doric column, designed by Benjamin Green (perhaps from his brother's earlier design), was begun in September 1837 and completed in August 1838 when the 13ft high statue of Grey, sculpted by Edward Hodges Baily was brought to the town from London aboard the Newcastle trading ship, *Halcyon*, and winched into position.[18]

At the foot of Grey Street, meanwhile, the old brick buildings defied the improving spirit and were still untouched when the Grainger transformation drew to its close in 1839. The buildings are thought to have been refronted to a design by John Dobson in 1842 but they remain, in part, an architectural anachronism.[19] This unfinished business was, however, against the run of play, for, overall in the five years up to 1839 Grainger was phenomenally successful in achieving the grand design he had first presented to the Common Council in May 1834. Long before the works were complete a report to the Corporation declared that Newcastle was "rapidly becoming one of the most splendid towns of the Kingdom."[20]

The views of a journalist, a historian and a traveller together summarise Richard Grainger's achievements in these years. The journalist Harriet Martineau, writing in 1840 – "Out of this has risen: nine new streets (exceeding collectively one mile and 289 yards), the new market, the Central Exchange, new theatre, new dispensary, music hall, lecture room, two chapels, incorporated company's hall, two auction marts, ten inns, twelve public houses, forty private houses and 325 houses with shops … the value of the property £800,000." Taking into account his previous works, the journalist observed that "nearly a million pounds has been added to the value of the town by one man in five years."[21] The historian Judge Lyall Wilkes writing in the 1960s – "this was a unique planning pioneering effort because it made Newcastle the first city with an elegantly planned commercial centre

"We cannot but admire the graceful curve of the course which adds so much to the beauty of the street and causes various points of architectural interest to gradually unfold as we proceed." Grainger's new streets became the focus of attention for illustrators and writers alike. Views of Grey Street captured its width, sweep and elegance but also its activity and bustle. The speed at which the new streets became the economic centre of the town was testimony to the market for commercial properties which Grainger had astutely identified.

The lower view (c.1841) shows the addition of a further property to the contentious south-east end of the street constructed in the intervening period.

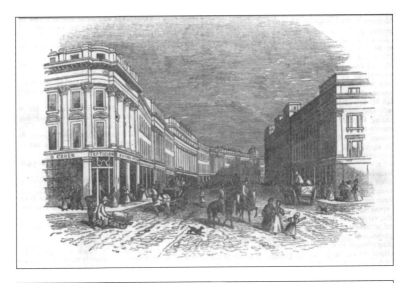

Before 1834, Wood of Bath had built graceful crescents, Adam had built squares in Edinburgh, Carr had built his houses in York, but Grainger's and Clayton's development was not of houses or public buildings, but of gracious shops and shopping arcades … in the Georgian style with ornate pillars, pilasters, pediments and friezes based òn the designs of classical Greek architecture. It was not only a unique achievement in 1834; in scale and beauty it has never been equalled in this country."[22] Finally, the traveller, William Howitt, in the early 1840s – "There is nothing like it in any history of any age … Before the magic of Mr Grainger, not merely have stone and timber become ductile and pliant, but the stony hearts and horny ideas of bankers, assurance brokers and capitalists in general, have melted and run down before him in streams of superabundant gold … Newcastle is now one of the most remarkable towns of the British Empire."[23]

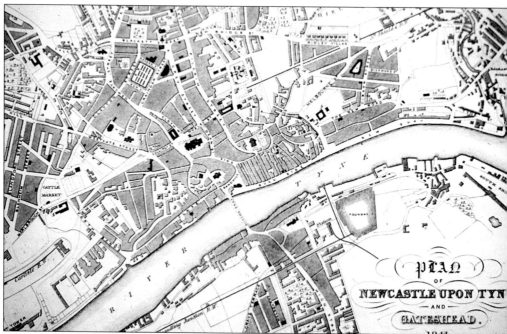

(above) **Grainger Street, c.1841. Collard after J.W. Carmichael**
Like Grey Street, Grainger Street reaches a geographical and architectural climax at the foot of Grey's Monumen
"It is" said Charleton, "handsome in its architecture but tame in comparison to Grey Street."

(below) **Plan of Newcastle, 1844 by Thomas Oliver**
Thomas Oliver's second plan records the effect of Grainger's redevelopment on the centre and the continuing
expansion of the town. Still to reach the period of positive explosion in the second half of the Victorian period, th
contrast with Oliver's first map is nevertheless marked.

# 10    Lofty and Modern Mansions

Notwithstanding that in 1889 John Clayton claimed to have suggested the all important curve in Grey Street modelled it was said on High Street, Oxford,[1] there seems little doubt that Richard Grainger was responsible for not only building the new centre of the town but also planning the outline of the scheme and the broad approach to its contents. However, the architecture which formed such a dominant aspect of the proposal was the result of Grainger combining his genius for strategy and implementation with the professional skills of the growing number of architects at work in the town.

Whilst in these years the town boasted what has been called the "strongest team of architects ever to be working at one time in Newcastle,"[2] attitudes within the profession as to the design of buildings were reaching a hiatus. Calling for an individual style for the times – an architecture of the period – was a rising refrain.[3] As the boundaries of knowledge and progress were being pushed forward at alarming rates in science, engineering and industry, the response of architects was to seek inspiration in the past, to look to the smooth, clean and uniform lines and disciplines of Classical Greek forms to counterbalance the surging and chaotic environment of the increasingly urbanised country. The classical designs for Grainger's developments not only provided elegance and style but also a solidity and dependability which offset the rapid pace of change which Grainger himself was generating. Not everyone was as comfortable with the style as the

The Queens Head Hotel, Grey Street. From *Shield Turner's Guide Book to Newcastle upon Tyne, 1846*

The Queen's Head is described as "one of the first Posting Houses in the Kingdom".

## REMOVAL TO GREY STREET.

## W. W. TEMPLE

HAS the honour most respectfully to announce to the nobility, gentry, his friends and the public of Newcastle, and the adjoining counties, that he has entered, for the Winter Trade, upon his New and Splendid Premises in Grey Street, which for *Elegance, Convenience and Comfort*, he ventures to hope *cannot be surpassed by any Establishment in the Kingdom.* In making so extensive a change, no time can be so well suited to return his best thanks to those kind friends, to whom so large a debt of gratitude is due, for the distinguished preference they have afforded him during his residence in Mosley Street,

**Clayton Street, 1910**

At its northern end, Clayton Street was designed to bring the great works at Eldon Square directly into the new street pattern, at its southern end to link, by extension, to the streets and houses of the Westgate area. Architecturally more work-a-day than the pomp of the other streets it has always retained a more populist air.

Tyneside classicists, some described it as "formal dullness", one archite wished that "the temples of Greece had long ago perished if the study them is to supersede all invention on our part."[4] The conflicting tradition one of which required the faithful following of classical examples and o based on innovation and individuality, created a battle of styles betwee Greek and Gothic architecture which dogged the early Victorian period. the redevelopment of Newcastle in these still early years of the centur however, the style was unreservedly classical.

That the roots of the architects who worked on Grainger's scheme la firmly in the Georgian tradition was in part due to the dynastic nature of th profession in this period. John Dobson had learned his profession with Dav Stephenson, in turn Thomas Oliver was a pupil of Dobson, Benjamin Gree and his brother John, junior, learned and practised with their father Joh Green. Andrew Oliver spent his early years in the profession in the office o the Greens. This was a small but influential circle, the talents of who

**Hood Street, c. 1912**

Although not gaining the same levels of attention and praise, the streets which linked the main thoroughfares were also carefully planned. Hood Street by 1912 had developed a blackened, less prosperous appearance but its underlying quality could not be denied.

Grainger was careful to utilise in converting his overall design into the quality of buildings befitting his vision.

Grainger, himself, was not a trained architect. When, in later years, he was asked by the Cholera Commissioners if he was a "builder and architect" he replied that he was.[5] Trade directories of the 1830s refer to him as an architect and on his death the Town Council Proceedings called him "one of the greatest architects of his age."[6] However, where professional men were gathered together, as in the Chamber of Commerce, he was careful not to present himself in this manner.[7] Nevertheless there was no doubting that he was keenly interested in the subject. The report of the Cholera Commission of 1854 noted that "he had a taste for art."[8] He, himself, observed that "I have decorated the houses (in the new town centre) in the manner you see and I was not obliged to do that … all the decoration that you see has been done because I was pleased to do it."[9] His interest may have been commercial, obtaining higher rents from more prestigious buildings, or may have stemmed from the general air of artistic and architectural advancement in the town which had begun in the 1770s. He, himself, attributed much to a visit to Edinburgh in his early years which he said had given him a strong delight and a powerful impulse – he was also later to visit London and Dublin. Architect or no, contemporary reports stress that he was responsible for all the essential points of design and that the architects he employed within his architectural department were "under Mr Grainger's immediate directions."[10]

Grainger, however, was far too astute not to allow his designers scope to develop their designs within his overall proposals. The result was architecture which matched the grandiose scale and majesty of the plan

**Grainger Street, 1917**

The heavier retail bias of Grainger Street and the later construction of Grainger Street West would ensure that its popularity would not wain. Trams also maintained the vibrancy of the thoroughfare which even in the middle years of the Great War was still busy.

itself. The basic design principle was to build in ranges, generally of two a[?] a half stories, decorated to varying degrees with columns, pilaster[?] pediments and balustrades.

"The fundamental design of the facades in every range," observed th[?] authors of *Tyneside Classical* "is based on either a central unit connecte[?] with the end or corner units by a simply designed straight facade – as [?] Hood Street, Grainger Street and the west side of Grey Street – [?] individually designed buildings integrated into the general sweep of a rang[?] as in Nelson Street and the east side of Grey Street."[11]

To implement his proposals Grainger employed two office architects [?] undertake the majority of the scheme and brought in the expertise of th[?] architectural elite to work on some of the larger or more distinct aspects [?] the development. Much of the credit for the architecture of the new tow[?] centre lies with John Wardle and George Walker who worked directly f[?] Grainger. Wardle and Walker were responsible for the design of a large pa[?] of Grey Street, Grainger Street, Market Street and Clayton Street as well [?] the impressive Central Exchange. Their names appear jointly on plans b[?] their individual contribution is difficult to determine. Wardle may have bee[?] the architect for the exterior of the new market. The market is general[?] assumed to have been the work of John Dobson and indeed a lithographe[?] view and a plan of the whole works "taken from the drawings of Joh[?] Dobson"[12] was available to the public at the time, but at the great banquet [?] mark its opening Grainger thanked his architect Wardle, making no mentio[?] of Dobson other than as the designer of its two large fountains. In a comme[?]

**Market Street, 1935**

Commercially the opening out of large stores, notably Bainbridge's, was the key to the success of many streets. Usually, however, their success lay in their combined effect – the long self-contained symmetrical blocks, and the use of conventional architectural forms on all the streets gave a pervading atmosphere of style and prosperity which could not be gainsaid by grime or Jubilee bunting.

to an inquiry into an accident on Market Street in 1835 Dobson, himself, only observed that he was engaged in superintending part of the erections around the new market. Dobson is, however, known to have drawn up the plans for the eastern side of Grey Street from Shakespeare Street to Mosley Street.[13] George Walker was involved in a whole range of designs including the Bank of England, the Central Exchange, the proposed Town Assizes, the Cordwainer's Hall, the Music Hall and many others. Grey's Monument, the Theatre Royal and the surrounding block including the north side of Shakespeare Street were the work of John and Benjamin Green. The Salem Chapel and part of Hood Street were designed by John Green, junior.[14] Others appear to have had lesser parts in the production. When the inquest into the death of six workmen resulting from a collapse of three houses on the south side of Market Street in June 1835 was held, Wardle and the Greens were called to give evidence, as were Mr Peter Nicholson, architect, a by then ageing but highly significant figure in the profession who had set up a School of Architecture in Newcastle in 1832[15] and Andrew Oliver, then an assistant to the Greens but in the following month to set up his own practice.[16] Andrew Oliver's involvement in Grainger's scheme is little known but an advertisement of 1838 refers to a new shop in Grey Street "executed from the design and under the direction of Andrew Oliver."[17] Thomas Oliver, despite his recent collaboration with Grainger in the Leazes, seems to have had little if any involvement in the grand plan. It is, then, to the relatively unknown figures of John Wardle and George Walker that most of the credit belongs for the startling architecture which rose in the new

**The Central Exchange
Reading Room, c.1880**

The interior of the
Central Exchange before
it was damaged by fire
in 1901, showing the
reading room in use as a
picture gallery. The
historian Charleton in
1888 promoted its use as
a permanent public art
gallery " … where the
tired citizen may look in
and, while resting, drink
in the beauties which art
lays before him." By
1897 the news room was
being used as a
Vaudeville Theatre but
from 1870 to 1895 the
Central Exchange
Gallery was an
important aspect of the
cultural life of
Newcastle.

streets. The Corporation had merely asked for buildings of "polished stone" instead they received "lofty and modern mansions" a "city of palaces".

The brightest jewel was Grey Street, since variably described as "one of the noblest and most magnificent streets," (Howitt)[18] "one of the best streets in England" (Pevsner)[19] and "England's finest street." (W. E. Gladstone) On it stood many of the noblest achievements: – the ten bay centrepiece of the lower west range designed for the Bank of England in the style of a "grand palazzo"; the massive frontage of the Turks Head Hotel; and, across the road, Green's Theatre Royal, "one of the largest and most beautiful outside of London … one of the greatest ornaments to Grey Street"; the (now Lloyds) bank, built utilising some of the designs for the ill-fated Courthouse scheme; and the Central Exchange – "a rich and beautiful semicircular building imbedded in a triangle of noble houses."[21] Together with the market, the largest in England with its splendid bazaar of shops and the sober and untheatrical architecture of the other streets, the value added to the town was not only financial but also aesthetic – a lasting legacy which owed its existence to "the spirit and enterprise of Mr Grainger."

# 11 The Link Snaps

T he success of Grainger's redevelopment was a product of his own drive and ability linked to the prudent use of others' skill, influence, and most importantly, money. The role of John Clayton in particular in this respect was crucial. There were, however, as there are today, national trends, influences and factors which helped to determine the course of events. Just as the late 1960s and early 70s presented the political, economic and social climate for Newcastle's Eldon Square Shopping Development, and the 1980s similarly for the Gateshead MetroCentre, so the mid-1830s were a time of considerable potential, particularly for the type of building speculation and development at which Grainger excelled.

On the back of one of the driving forces of the economy – the expanding railway industry – an investment boom was building which peaked in 1836.[1] Whilst directed principally at the many opportunities which the new and rapidly growing rail network presented, investment capital became more available as land and mineral owners, in particular, sought to put their money to work. This situation was reflected in the growth and development of the banking system through the nineteenth century and by the rise of the 'businessman'. At the same time the growing urbanisation of the country was creating a market for town centre facilities on a scale previously unheard of. The demand for properties for shops was growing greatly in this period. As towns did away with the medieval markets they built new covered facilities and specialised shops, and also became home to the developing department stores, Bainbridge's for example which was founded in 1838. As the economy shook off its reliance on the vagaries of the weather and the harvest and the proportion of the urban population joining the 'middle classes' grew, the role of not only the professions in their town-based offices – lawyers, architects, insurance agents, bankers and the like – but also of the gentlemen's outfitters, milliners, haberdashers and suppliers of other goods

GENTLEMEN desirous of having a Hat of the newest Shape, the most tastefully executed, and at an amazingly reduced Price, can have their Wishes realized by purchasing at
**W. WINGRAVE'S**
THE MANUFACTURER, GRAINGER STREET,
NEWCASTLE UPON TYNE,

NORTHUMBERLAND TEA AND COFFEE MARTS

DAVID GIBSON,
Tea Coffee and Spice Merchant.
18, Grainger St NEWCASTLE on TYNE.

expanded. These were the people and the organisations who moved int
Grainger's new streets almost as quickly as he built them.

The speed with which Grainger built was also symptomatic of a nation
trend. The building trade throughout the country was the most rapid
expanding area of employment. Although the demand for new building
grew, the techniques employed in building them were still largely based
antiquity. To this day the construction of traditional family houses is a
labour-intensive as it has been for centuries. A prerequisite for th
implementation of the town centre redevelopment was therefore th
availability of a large workforce. That Grainger was able to employ 2,0(
men was made possible by the rising population of the area, the intern
migration within it and possibly an early but small influx of Irish laboure
into the area.[2] The number nevertheless represented a staggeringly larg
proportion of the local workforce. The building industry was, as to a less
degree it still is, prone to heavy seasonal fluctuations – in February 183
soup kitchens were set up in Newcastle because of the severity of the seaso
and the general suspension of labour[3] – and greatly affected by periods
economic prosperity and recession. When projects were launched therefo
large workforces could be assembled and the speed of construction could b
breakneck. In late Victorian London it was said that "houses sprang up as
in a single night, streets in a month, churches and chapels in a quarter."[4]

These were some of the national trends which underpinned Grainger
planning and construction of a purely commercial centre. However, whil
these formed the backdrop to the developments more direct influences an
local individuals were particularly instrumental in ensuring the success c

**hn Clayton (1792-
90)**

ayton's influence on
th Grainger and
wcastle was threefold
as the Town Clerk for
considerable term
822-67), as one of its
ding solicitors and as
nan of considerable
tune. His role in
ging the link between
ainger's ambition, the
pital of leading men
d large institutions
d the needs and
sires of the Town and
Corporation was
votal to the success of
e redevelopment of
e town centre.

the transformation. The support of John Clayton was perhaps the most important single factor in securing the redevelopment of the town centre.[5]

When Grainger's schemes came to encompass the transformation of a large part of the town his solicitor, financial adviser and mentor John Fenwick suggested that Grainger might transfer his business matters to the care of John Clayton's practice, then perhaps the wealthiest, largest and most prestigious legal firm in the town. Clayton, whose father Nathaniel had been a prime mover in the improvements to the town in the 1780s, was, furthermore, Town Clerk and had considerable influence with the Common Council – an important factor in the eventual agreement of the Council to Grainger's plan. However, despite Clayton's backing Grainger was unable to carry the Council with him in his two attempts to provide a Corn Market, nor was he able to get his own way with the proposals to build a new Courthouse, nor secure permission to extend Grainger Street. It would seem that Clayton's influence did not outweigh the interests of the Council members, and it is perhaps not in his role as Town Clerk but as Grainger's solicitor and adviser, that the true importance of Clayton's involvement lies. A complex array of property deals lay at the heart of all Grainger's activities. The methods with which he financed his proposals were sinuous. Legal advice and expertise were essential to the success of his enterprises. Even

**The Plan of the two designs for the new corn market. From a letter to *The Tyne Mercury* (18th September, 1837)**

Grainger had already been rebuffed once in proposing to erect a new corn market and had instead built the Royal Arcade, the debate was still unresolved when he offered, again without success, the triangular site at the head of Grey Street and Grainger Street as an alternative to the Council's favoured location in Middle Street.

Laing Art Gallery

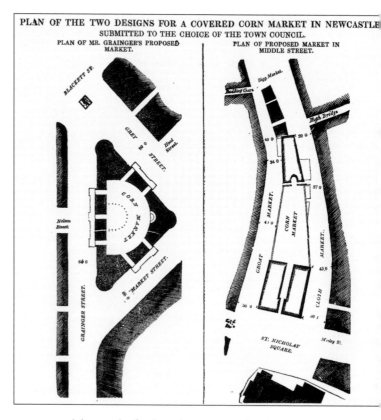

PLAN OF THE TWO DESIGNS FOR A COVERED CORN MARKET IN NEWCASTLE SUBMITTED TO THE CHOICE OF THE TOWN COUNCIL.

PLAN OF MR. GRAINGER'S PROPOSED MARKET.

PLAN OF PROPOSED MARKET IN MIDDLE STREET.

more essential were the funds and contacts which Clayton could open up the increasingly ambitious Grainger.

From his earliest ventures Richard Grainger had been able to attract backing from connections he had made. In the first instance through the Methodist Movement he had not only secured work through Alderman Batson, established a valuable and influential link with John Fenwick but also met his well-connected wife Rachel. Whilst Batson had given Grainger his first major opportunity, it was Fenwick who forged important links with available money and for some years acted on behalf of Grainger in his transactions. Throughout his career Grainger worked on the principle of recycling cash and credit to finance his next scheme.[6] When he made the vital link with Clayton a wider door opened and the resources of not just wealthy individuals but also large institutions, such as the Northumberland District Banking Company became available. During his early development he could perhaps have broken the chain and secured for himself a very presentable fortune, but as he reached further, the levels of investment, mortgage values and rents rose allowing yet more purchases of property and yet more development but yet more risk until, as the authors of Tyneside Classical put it, "a link snapped or time ran out."[7]

Recent research has shown that the key element in the financial arrangements upon which Grainger was able to arrange the purchase

Anderson Place was a system known as Lease and Release. This allowed Grainger, and the Corporation, the opportunity to pay the £50,000 price for the property in instalments, and gave the time to earn back some of the investment money in leases before either the full cost had to be met or later payments became due.[8] Many other property deals took place using this system or involving what amounted to Compulsory Purchase Orders by the Corporation. It is clear that Grainger relied to a large extent on wealthy backers whose credit at some point had to be met from increasingly larger proposals.

To meet his growing repayments and to fulfil his own desire to develop the town, even during the implementation of his plan for the town centre, Grainger was not idle in looking for new opportunities. In offering the town new Law Courts in the plot of ground north of the Theatre he had offered to take in return either a sum of money (£28,000) or the sites of various properties in the town – including the Guildhall – which held development potential. In the same vein he offered to convert the Moot Hall for commercial purposes. Similarly in his attempts to convince the Council that the Exchange Buildings he was erecting would form the Corn Market they had sought for almost a decade he suggested in a letter to the Corporation the potential development opportunities which might accrue from the demolition of archaic properties in the Bigg Market, Groat Market and Middle Street area.[9] Perhaps resulting from the rebuttal of these proposals, however, he turned his attention to a part of the town where his room for manoeuvre was not restricted by uncooperative landowners or interested parties within the Corporation, and bought on 2nd January 1839 the Elswick Estate of John Hodgson Hinde.[10]

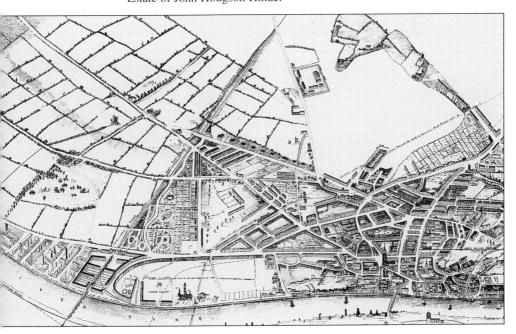

**Elswick Hall. c.1935**

The purchase of a fine country mansion was the traditional culmination to the amassing of a great fortune. Richard Grainger was certainly a man of considerable standing and investments but neither his wealth nor his proposals for the site were based on traditional foundations. The failure of Grainger's Elswick venture represented an unhappy meeting between new and old ways.

The Elswick Estate which extended northwards from the riverside to west of the town was developed in the seventeenth century by a weal Newcastle merchant. John Hodgson rebuilt Elswick Hall which stood at centre of the Estate in 1803 to designs by William and John Stokoe.[11] (T hall was demolished in 1980 and the site is now occupied by the Elsw Swimming Pool). John Hodgson Hinde inherited the estate in 1820. Member of Parliament with a keen interest in the town, he was willing to s the Estate and Hall to the ambitious Grainger for £114,000. Grainger bou the Estate as a speculative opportunity, but he bought the Hall in order to l in a manner befitting the maker of modern Newcastle.

With this purchase, however, the "link snapped". His contin reinvestment of capital, the colossal expenditure on the town cen improvement, exacerbated perhaps by the £100,000 which he later said l been the cost of the decoration he had added to the buildings to dignify a glorify the town, meant that he had little capital of his own. Approximat £104,000 of the purchase price was loaned from banks, adding furth repayment demands to his already unsteady position. Grainger envisaged the grounds of the 800 acre estate the development of what today would known as an industry or business park. Large factories would be built railway terminus and a shipping quay would form the all important transp links and housing would grow up on the pleasant higher ground and himself would live with his family in the splendour of Elswick Hall.

This was, in many ways, a very far seeing scheme which preda

Armstrong's colonisation of the site, the replacement of the eighteenth century Tyne Bridge with the Swing Bridge and the formation of the railway and shipping links which were so fundamental to the development of Tyneside in the second half of the nineteenth century. However, only a small area of the proposed housing was successfully completed before the financial roof fell in on him. Graingerville South – the terrace of eight sandstone ashlar houses on the south side of Westgate Road – stands as testimony to the potential and proposed quality of Grainger's last great venture. However, speculative housing in itself was not the road to financial salvation, nor was it the type of development upon which Grainger's reputation and success had been built. Only months after the effective conclusion of his town centre works, not much more than a year after the celebratory dinner in the Central Exchange, he found himself facing the prospect of financial ruin.

If any single event triggered Grainger's financial collapse is not clear, but from 1839 there is an increasingly hectoring tone to the letters to him from his solicitors asking for payments which, in the context, were relatively trifling sums.[12] By November of 1839 not only were there increasing calls for the meeting of payments but also complaints from the Town Improvement Committee, particularly regarding the state of the streets which Grainger had agreed to maintain but were rapidly deteriorating.[13] John Clayton was already trying to "prevent unpleasant proceedings".[14] Grainger's inability to meet payments and to fulfil his promises to the Corporation led to him spending several days in the custody of the Sheriff in August 1841.[15] On his release, further demands from the Town Improvement Committee followed and one of his creditors threatened to commence bankruptcy proceedings. He fled the town and spent the period from mid-September to November in a self-imposed exile which saw him first in Liverpool, then Penrith, then the Queensbury Arms, Annan and finally Edinburgh. In these havens he stubbornly ignored the entreaties of Clayton to return and accept the negotiated agreement which he (Clayton) had reached which would at least allow Grainger an annual income of £300 whilst his debts and financial affairs were placed principally in the control of his major creditors.[16] Grainger's unwillingness to return to Newcastle and face the music was the cause of mounting frustration for Clayton who was moved to write to Grainger that "the idea that you can escape from them by not returning home, allow me to say, is perfectly childish."[17] Clayton's exasperation was heightened by Grainger's taciturn behaviour over the loss of the furniture and fittings of Elswick Hall, the sale of which had been arranged with Christian Allhusen, a leading chemicals manufacturer, who visited the mansion on Christmas Day, 1841, to complete the transfer of its contents. Grainger's unwillingness to relinquish the hall and its contents was similarly baffling – an "Act of Madness" – to Clayton who was taking great pains to preserve Grainger from the ignominy of being publicly declared bankrupt. "There is no disposition on the part of any Friends of yours to turn

**Clayton Street West, Residence of Mr Grainger, 1843. From** *Sketches Illustrative of the Life of Richard Grainger* **by John Green**

Grainger spent the final two decades of his life living at 5 Clayton Street West and working in his office at the neighbouring No.9. The buildings are now renumbered as 36 and 28 Clayton Street West.

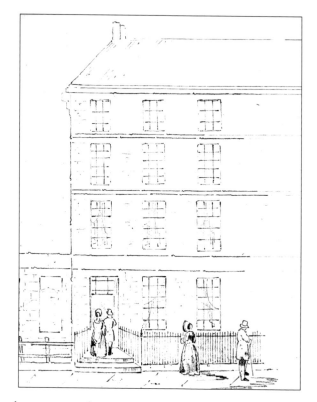

their backs on you, unless you turn your back on yourself" he wrote. Grainger's attempts to offset the disaster by selling off property failed f want of buyers[19] and at the end of January 1842 he was forced to pri himself and his family away from his ill-fated occupation of Elswick Ha He removed himself to the residence he was to occupy for the rest of his li at 5 Clayton Street West and carried on his depleted business from t neighbouring property of 9 Clayton Street West. The care of the new street by 1841 in a "most deplorable condition",[20] was taken on by t Corporation's Town Improvement Committee but Grainger's credito continued to press for payment. Clayton skilfully engineered an arrangeme whereby the principal debts were met by the sale of half of the Elswic estate, whilst the rest of the property was vested in the name of Grainger eldest son, Thomas Charles Grainger, thus ensuring that a part of Grainger investment was safeguarded and that his town centre investments were n lost.[21] John Clayton prevented the stigma of failure and bankruptcy fallir upon his friend's head, but whilst the Grainger estate would in time becom very valuable as property values soared in the latter half of the nineteent century, at the time of his death in 1861 Richard Grainger's debts st exceeded £128,000 whilst his personal estate amounted to less tha £17,000.[22]

# The Genius of Mr Grainger

Financial difficulties dogged the years following Grainger's departure from Elswick Hall. Two years later a large number of his creditors remained unpaid, but the selling off of large swathes of the Elswick Estate and the financial machinations of John Clayton allowed Grainger to live in a comfortable, if not opulent, manner and to carry on his business in a reduced and financially less cavalier manner. The experience of the previous few years were a bitter blow to a man who such a short time ago had been feted, honoured and acclaimed and was seemingly at the height of his power and achievements. His unwillingness to accept the change in circumstances as illustrated in the "acts of Madness", the "childish" behaviour and his refusal to leave his Elswick home until the very last moment, is perhaps understandable. These were certainly not characteristics which contemporary observers associated with the man in his prime.

**Richard Grainger from a watercolour by David Mossman (1825-1901)**

Portrayed in his later years he sits, once again, with the head of Grey Street visible through the window – perhaps purposefully showing the area where Anderson Place once stood.

Lent by R. Wilson to the Laing Art Gallery

Harriet Martineau declared that as a child, Grainger "was the remarkable for nothing but his serenity, his characteristic through life", youth of far-seeing vision who dreamed of achieving the transformation of the town, who as an apprentice "won some attention by the remarkable steadiness and easy composure of his character, giving promise of respectability and indications of power of mind." In his early years of business he had "inspired his neighbours with a strong confidence in his integrity." The journalist's rose-tinted view of Grainger added that he had "strong principles of self-control. Grainger was never seen out of temper, nor does his quiet cheerfulness ever appear to give way, it is clear that something far beyond common good nature has been the means of bringing him through without injury to his health or peace of mind. He is very popular among his men, finding leisure to consider their interests and pleasure in extending his generosity to their families."[1] Other observers were keen to stress his calmness and his perseverance, his dynamism and confidence ("The word 'impossible' does not find entrance into his vocabulary" opined the Reverend Dibdin[2]), others his humbleness, modesty and diffidence. Even allowing for an element of journalistic hyperbole, this amounts to a list of characteristics which is hard to equate with the hard-headed approach he would have had to take to achieve his objectives.

For all his achievements, the private man was and is still little known. Grainger was not a gregarious character. At a time when a man's worth was measured by his standing among his peers, Grainger does not seem to have involved himself in the cultural or learned societies of the town or embroiled himself in the political milieu. Although a member, but not an officer, of the Chamber of Commerce, his name does not occur on lists of patrons or members of less commercially orientated organisations. He was, however, willing to look kindly on the establishment of Botanical and Zoological Gardens on his Elswick estate[3] and in later life he arranged for sums of money to be given on his death to St Andrew's Free School for Boys, the Infirmary, Newcastle Dispensary, Victoria Blind Asylum, the Society for the Relief of Married Women Lying-In at Home and the Northern Asylum for the Deaf and Dumb.[4] His attitude toward the political arena was expressed in a handbill he produced in 1835, one of his few public declarations answering insinuations of political transgressions "I had never interfered in politics" he said "nor do I intend to do so."[5] The suggestion that he was an avuncular employer was somewhat belied by his treatment of striking workers: "We remember on one of the first of these occasions [suggesting there must have been others], the excitement in the town at the news that Grainger's men had struck and the curiosity to see what he would do. There he was in the midst of his stone and timber, as serene as a summer morning secure in his plans. Before the evening he had sworn in six hundred apprentices. Being asked what he would do with so many novices, he answered that his excavations were just then his chief object, and the boys

TO THE

# BURGESSES

OF

## SAINT ANDREW'S SOUTH WARD.

### Gentlemen,

I have this Moment seen a Handbill, in which I am stigmatised as interfering in a Matter in which I have no Concern, and as acting at the instigation of another. My offence is, the Endeavour to forward the Return of fit and proper Representatives in the Council, for a Ward in which, though it may happen that I am not registered as a Burgess, yet in which I may venture to say that no one has a greater Stake than myself; and I need the instigation of no one to induce me to use my utmost exertions to promote its interests.

It is but an act of justice to the Gentleman whose Name the writer of this handbill is pleased to introduce on this occasion, and who, it is well known, has studiously refrained from any interference, to state the fact, that much as I value that Gentleman's opinion (and the opinion of so true a friend to the interests of the Town, is, I admit, entitled to great Weight), I never thought of asking it on the present Occasion ; and when it was suggested by him to me, as a measure of prudence, to refrain from taking any part in the approaching election, I replied to him, as I reply to this anonymous writer,—" That I had never interfered in politics, nor did I intend to do so; but that no one could blame me, interested as I was in the prosperity of the Town, for exerting myself to secure the return of fit and proper men, as I deemed Mr Alderman Bell and Mr Alderman Brandling to be, as Members of the Council."

I will not condescend to notice the Insinuation that I have other Objects to answer, further than by assuring my Fellow-Townsmen that I have no " Matters to settle with the New Council," or with any one else, which I shrink from submitting to any tribunal.

I am, Gentlemen,

Your faithful Servant,

**Richard Grainger.**

Leazes Terrace, December 24, 1835.

could excavate under his directions. So they did; the men offered themselves in crowds again presently. He picked and chose from among them – those whom he rejected being left at leisure to bewail their strike."[6] At a time when labour relations were coming to the forefront of economic considerations in the North East mining industry and unionism was making early strides, Grainger's reaction was perhaps not an unusual response, but it serves to illustrate a ruthless side to his nature.

The overriding characteristic of all Grainger's work was its commercialism. His developments did not include any elements of philanthropy, he did not build housing for the less well-off or look to the provision of social facilities, but at the same time went to great pains to dignify the town with an architectural approach which was more elaborate

**High Level Bridge, Newcastle by George Henry Andrews, 1872**

The task of designing a new bridge at high level in to the town in the 1840s exercised the minds of many leading engineers, architects and builders. At least nineteen different proposals were put forward, including ones from Isambard Kingdom Brunel, Robert Stephenson, John Green, John Dobson and Richard Grainger. The chosen design was that of Robert Stephenson, the bridge being completed in 1849. Bringing rail traffic into the new Central Station and road traffic into the town at high level the bridge had a marked effect on the development of the town.

Laing Art Gallery

than it needed to be. Similarly the sanitary provisions for his buildings were exemplary and the arrangements for water and gas supply to the new streets were progressive, but also commercially based – he laid the pipes and then looked to strike deals with the supply companies.[7] He was first and foremost a man of business. His standards seem to have been high. In all his major construction works there were only two serious accidents – a collapse of scaffolding at the Leazes and the building collapse in Market Street. Martineau says that "Gentlemen who have had to receive periodical payments from him declare him to be the most regular payer they ever had to do with"[8] – a view which is not totally borne out by the tone of some of John Clayton's correspondence with Grainger. As to his probity in these matters there are few indicators. He was obliged to issue the statement in 1835 denying any underhand involvement in political decisions, and during the debate over the provision of new law courts allegations of corruption and insinuations regarding his motives were made.[9] However, in the context of a still oligarchic Council with considerable vested interests, that so few allegations were made against a man of such considerable achievement is perhaps a testimony in itself, bringing to mind the words of Lord Clive " I stand astonished at my own moderation."[10]

Moderation, however, was not an adjective which could be applied to Grainger's business approach. His continual expansion of his credit when he could have cashed in the copious amount of money accrued from some of his early developments and lived in considerable luxury, as advised by others reflects his ambitious nature – the characteristic which eventually led Grainger to over-reach himself. Even in the years following his difficulties he proposed schemes which were, if not on the scale of his town centre redevelopment or his dreams for the Elswick estate, still nevertheless

substantial. He once again attempted to persuade the Council to extend Grainger Street to the new railway station and offered to include in his proposals the provision of sewers and the paving and flagging of the street. He formulated a plan to supply the town with water and he also contributed to the numerous plans to construct what was to become the High Level Bridge. His bridge proposal showed, for him, a curious lack of foresight, catering only for road and foot traffic and making no provision for the railway.[11] It was not that he misunderstood the importance of the railway – in 1836 he had formulated a plan to bring together the termini of three railways in Newcastle. His proposed new bridge would have linked directly into the foot of Mosley Street and thereby into his own town centre. This and his other larger plans came to nought but he continued in business to the end. On the day of his death he was "engaged up to half past ten o'clock in the morning issuing orders to his employees."[12] He died suddenly at 12.30 p.m. on Thursday, 4th July 1861, aged 64, from "disease of the heart." A fortnight previously he had been confined indoors as a result of a sprained leg but had spent part of the previous week at Tynemouth "in his usual health, enjoying the sea breeze and fine weather."[13] His sudden death came as a considerable shock to his family and to the people of the town.

His family have scarcely featured in this story of Grainger's life and achievements and yet, in direct contrast to John Clayton who remained a bachelor throughout his considerable lifetime, Grainger had a typically large Victorian family. His mother had died in January 1835 at the age of eighty. His wife Rachel, in the early years of their marriage, had been involved in Richard's business affairs and was described as "an excellent wife who possessed good taste and was a good business and accounts manager"[14] but her involvement diminished as the web of intricate finance grew wider and the levels of investment and credit expanded to a point where legal and financial matters became intertwined. Moreover her time became devoted to the increasing size of their family. Their first son, Thomas Charles, was born on 6th April 1822, seven months from the date of their marriage. In the course of their nineteen-year marriage they had thirteen children – six sons and seven daughters.[15] Rachel Grainger died at Lanark on the 16th October 1842 giving birth to their final child Henry Benjamin who died just a few days later – a double tragedy which, coming so soon after his financial crash, must mark the darkest days of Richard Grainger's life. Only Joseph, of the four sons who reached maturity, married but his marriage was without issue. The eldest Thomas Charles became involved in the family business in the wake of the Elswick disaster and inherited his father's estate on Richard's death. In his will, written in October 1857, Richard Grainger left £1,000 to each of his daughters and £2,000 to each of his sons.[16]

On the death of Thomas Charles Grainger on 9th February 1884 the estate was left to his nephew Henry Liddell, who in the terms of the will was

**Rachel Grainger, wife of Richard Grainger, c.1830**

Mrs Grainger, painted by the same unknown artist as her husband, probably as a pair, when Grainger came to prominence. She was the daughter of Joseph Arundale, a wealthy businessman in the leather trade. She married Richard in October 1821 and bore him six sons and seven daughters. She died in October 1842 in childbirth. Harriet Martineau described her as "an excellent wife who possessed good taste and was a good business and accounts manager."

Laing Art Gallery

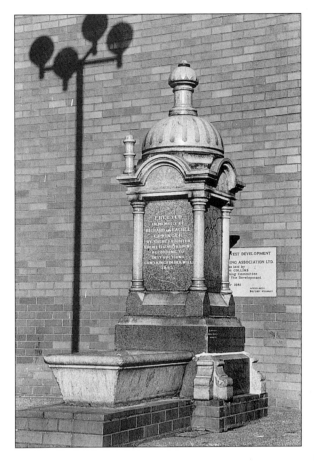

**The Grainger Memorial Drinking Fountain in Waterloo Street**

Removed to its present site from a position in Neville Street in the 1950s, the trough and drinking fountain was erected in Memory of Richard and Rachel Grainger by their daughter Rachel Elizabeth Burns according to instructions in her will" The monument is dated 1892 and signed "Elswick Court Marble Works Co. Newcastle."

Photo: Dave Hewitt

to take the name and arms of Grainger after reaching the age of thirty-five.[17] By this time the debts of the estate had long since been met and rising property values had created the type of wealth which perhaps should have come to a man who gave so much to his town. Clayton's continued work to resolve the tangled web of finances and later the equally tireless contribution of William Gibson of Clayton and Gibson, ensured that his investments prospered. By the turn of the twentieth century the Grainger estate was worth over £1,200,000.[18] But it is not the monetary value of Grainger's work which was its lasting value. On his death he joined the pantheon of great men who had steered Newcastle and the North East to the dominating position it held in the high Victorian period – he had combined the rise from poverty and the achievement of George Stephenson with the skill and vision of Robert Stephenson; he stood with Armstrong in the effect he had had on the development of the town. He was one of the towering figures in the making of Newcastle.

When the news of his death was announced, "universal sorrow and regret" were felt in the town, the minute-bell of St Nicholas' tolled and shop-keepers put up their shutters as a mark of respect. He was laid to rest in the

family vault in Benwell Churchyard. A letter in the *Daily Journal* in 186
lamented the lack of gratitude displayed by the town in their failure to erec
a monument to Richard Grainger akin to those to Earl Grey and George
Stephenson – "a scandal and a shame."[19] This was a time when civi
achievements were marked by the erection of more mundane but practica
monuments such as clocks and drinking fountains. When statues of grea
men once again became fashionable at the turn of the century Richar
Grainger was long gone. Instead his grave, the name Grainger Street, a smal
public fountain and water trough, now standing in Waterloo Street bu
originally erected in Neville Street in 1892 – following an instruction in th
will of his daughter Rachel Elizabeth Burns[20] – and a plaque in St John
Church ("A Citizen of Newcastle does not need to be reminded of the geniu
of Richard Grainger and a stranger is referred to the principal street in th
centre of the city as forming the most splendid and enduring monument t
that genius") were, for over a hundred years, the only public monuments t
his role in the making of Newcastle. Fittingly a new monument to Richar
Grainger will soon grace the street which bears his name to mark th
bicentenary of his birth. The *Newcastle Daily Journal* on the day after hi
death, however, spoke for the people of the town by repeating the word
once dedicated to Christopher Wren – "If you seek my monument, loo
around."[21] At his funeral, which took place on Wednesday 10th July 186
attended by the Mayor and Corporation, his role in saving Newcastle "fror
the dilapidations of age" was acknowledged and acclaimed.[22] The tru
significance of his works, however, had been encapsulated in a comment i
the *Journal* in 1836 as the majesty of his streets unfolded "Newcastle is
town which is making more strides in wealth, population and importanc
than perhaps any other in the Empire."[23]

**Grey Street**

"A Citizen of Newcastle does not need to be reminded of the genius of Richard Grainger and a stranger is referred to the principal street in the centre of the city as forming the most splendid and enduring monument to that genius."

Photo: Dr Tom Yellowley

# 13 Grainger Town

Richard Grainger gave Newcastle a new heart, but the industrial, manufacturing and commercially based towns of the nineteenth century seldom stood still, even without the dynamic influences of men like Grainger. A key factor in the success of towns, and indeed whole regions, was their relationship with the increasingly vital railways. When the iron artery penetrated into the centre of Newcastle with the construction of the High Level Bridge and the opening of Central Station in 1850, it created an important focal point outside of Grainger's new centre. Moreover the high level road link which the new bridge provided saw the re-establishment of Newgate Street and Percy Street as alternative routes to the north, and forced the re-appraisal of the need to extend Grainger Street southwards – a scheme which was carried out, with an accompanying mish-mash of Gothic and eclectically designed offices and shops, in 1868.

Beyond the centre the spread of residential areas continued with the laying out of more middle-class terraces along the Great North Road.[1] Speculative builders threw up houses in all parts of the town. However the Health of Towns Commission of 1845 found the newly-built streets in both Gateshead and Newcastle to be as bad as the old – including those built in the 1840s in the Blenheim Street and Blandford Street area, an area of potential residential development which Grainger had identified in 1834. In contrast to the elegance and the facilities provided by Grainger, however, these were a disgrace to the town and disease was rife – "Typhus, fever, cholera or other epidemic diseases ought never to have existed in the neighbourhood and never would have done so but for the criminal cupidity of builders and the absence or non-enforcement of proper regulations," lamented one councillor, "from a desire to obtain the largest possible rental from the smallest possible surface, the whole of this backland has been filled up with inferior houses built up into narrow pestilential lanes and attempted to be dignified by the names of Temple Street, Peel Street, Westmoreland Place etc..."[2] The contrast between the nine elegant streets of Grainger and other areas of town was a common observation. In time these contrasts would be most marked in the mass of tightly packed streets which began to march up from the river banks to create the sprawling suburbs of Scotswood and Elswick. But in the first half of the century some of the worst parts of the town lay only a matter of yards from the splendid new centre. In the steep gorge created by the river, a miasma of smoke from factory chimneys and

**Aftermath of the Quayside Fire, 7th October 1854**

The wholesale redevelopment of the western end of the Quayside following the fire reduced the rate of decline of the lower parts of the town and reduced the stark contrast with Grainger's streets. The destruction of quayside properties in the fire was immense. This view (by Henry Brady) shows the lesser areas of damage at the east end of the Quay near Broad Chare.

steamboat stacks mingled with rank odours from alkali works and abatto the appalling stench of blood boiling and the malodorous burning of ho flesh and bones in the glue factories, to create a rancid atmosphere.[3] shock of the appalling cholera outbreak of 1853 which struck in Newca with particular severity, carrying away 1,533 victims, was still fresh in mind when the great fire of 1854, although causing death, mayhem a considerable loss of property, swept away some of the worst fever dens the town.[4]

Nor was the contrast a matter of physical appearance. The respecta and refined facade represented by Grainger's buildings and streets was reflected in other parts of the town. The Chief Constable's report for 18 identified 71 brothels and 46 houses of ill repute in the town. In 1854 th were more than 100 brothels and 500 public houses and beer shops Newcastle.[5] Earlier in the century Eneas McKenzie coyly observed that Quayside was a "dirty and inconvenient street" and that chares leading fr it were the "receptacle of Cyprian nymphs whose blandishments were of most coarse and vulgar description. Indeed most of these dark lanes w inhabited by very dangerous though not very tempting females."[6] On same day in 1837 that the Council considered Grainger's elegant Cen Exchange proposal, they also debated the value of scattering concentrating in one area of the town "all the lewd and disorderly houses The replacement of a large part of the disreputable properties of Quayside, following the fire, with the Dobson designed commercial grid streets – Queen Street, King Street and Lombard Street – was a major s in forming a more cohesive identity between the upper parts and the lo parts of the town. In truth, however, the importance of the quayside to commercial heart of the town declined markedly after the building of

**…ey Street, 1884**

…Triumphal Arch set …in Grey Street for the …yal Visit of the Prince …l Princess of Wales. …e route of the …cession testifies to …continuing quality of …y Street but by this …e it was no longer …premier street of the …n. Prince Albert …ward and his wife …nt on to open the new …k at North Shields, …event which would, …reducing the shipping …Newcastle Quayside, …o in time reduce the …portance of the streets …ich led to the river.

High Level Bridge and the construction of docks in the lower reaches of the Tyne. Gradually the significance of the riverside area to the prosperity of the town centre reduced. One of the effects of which was to lessen the importance of the Grey Street connection with Dean Street which, in Grainger's plan, had been a key link in establishing the importance of the new street. By the 1880s, then, Grey Street was no longer Newcastle's premier street.

By the late nineteenth century the newly-designated city had experienced an explosion in size and population – based to a large degree on the huge growth of the engineering and shipbuilding industries typified and led by the massive Armstrong works established on the land Grainger had once owned at Elswick riverside. The needs of the growing population were met by an expanding town centre. The new retail outlets of Grainger Street West and Northumberland Street, spearheaded by Fenwick's Department Store which opened in 1878, made these the main streets of the town. A

**Fenwick's Summer Sale, Northumberland Street, 1898**

The opening of Fenwick's Department Store in Northumberland Street in 1878 emphasised the movement of the commercial centre of the town away from Grainger's streets. By the time of the Summer Sale of 1898 crowds thronged Northumberland Street, the store and the balcony.

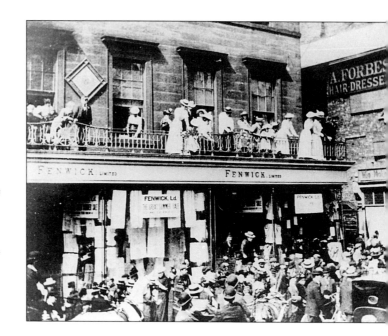

petition requesting the reduction of rates in Grey Street in the 1880s poin out that "Grey Street has lost its prestige as the leading commerc thoroughfare of Newcastle."[8] The replacement of the decaying building: Collingwood Street and Mosley Street with new offices for the major ba and insurance companies gave impetus to that part of the town[9] and extension of Market Street to New Bridge Street created further competit to the fading prosperity of Grainger's centre.

This state of affairs was compounded in the twentieth century by opening of the new Tyne Bridge in 1928 which re-established Pilgrim Str as the entrance to the town, a status which was confirmed and enhanced the building of a headquarters for the Newcastle Electric Supply Comp. in Carliol House, and the construction of magistrates courts, the pol station, the fire station and the council offices in the formerly dilapida street. Also confirmed was the role of Northumberland Street as the tow most important street, acting as both the nucleus for shopping and as par the main road to London and Edinburgh. Observers saw, however, only hard industrial face of the inter-war city. That the town no longer presen its best face to the visitor was evidenced as early as 1850. When Qu Victoria visited the town to open the new bridge and Station, she was sai be so appalled at what she saw that ever after, on passing through the tov she would have the curtains of her carriage drawn. Eighty years later J Priestley on his *English Journey* wrote: "A great bridge over a steam space and we were in Newcastle ... I have a very distinct recollection taking a great dislike to the whole district. The centre of Newcastle ha certain sombre dignity ... there are more impressive buildings than would expect. It is chiefly built of a stone that has turned almost a d black. Newcastle is even blacker than Manchester, and might almost have been carved out of coal." Priestley's view is perhaps tainted; he was certainly no lover of Tyneside, describing Gateshead as appearing to have been "carefully planned by an enemy of the human race ... no true civilisation could have produced such a town", whilst reserving his most stinging invective for Wallsend where he said "slatternly women stood at the doors of wretched little houses, gossiping with other slatterns or screeching for their small children who were playing among the filth of the roadside". Geordies as a whole he dismissed as "stocky, toothless fellows in caps and mufflers cursing in their uncouth accents."[10]

The very people Priestley was disparaging were, however, an important factor in the development of the city centre – their growing needs, linked to improved access to the city centre provided by buses, trams and the emerging popularity of the motor car, were changing the appearance of the centre – men (mostly) swarmed into the town to watch Newcastle United, families flooded into, particularly, Northumberland Street to shop. The town, in due course, developed an identifiable shopping area distinguishable from the streets dominated by offices. In time a third specialised area would grow up to the north of the town where the buildings of the older and newer Universities and the new Civic Centre would create an identifiable academic and administrative sector augmenting the shopping and business areas. Plans to control the development of the town had been produced in the inter-war period and in 1945 and 1951 but with little effect.[11]

It was, however, the implementation of the City Council's 1963 Development Plan, principally under the leadership of T. Dan Smith, which brought major changes to the city centre, laying out John Dobson Street to ease the pressure on Northumberland Street, developing the Central Motorway, redesigning the foot of Pilgrim Street and promoting a new shopping area north of Blackett Street. Time and hindsight has given these changes a mixed set of marks – the plan has been much maligned, but the Central Motorway, although felt by many to be too close to the centre of the town has largely solved the north-south traffic movement through the city and the Eldon Square Shopping Centre has been an undoubted commercial success. John Dobson Street, however, was certainly not a street with which the man himself would have wished to be associated and the pedestrian and architectural features of the Pilgrim Street roundabout have been perhaps the most vilified aspects of the whole city. Whilst Grainger's town centre escaped relatively unscathed from this modernisation, the principle casualties were two of Grainger's earlier masterpieces, the Royal Arcade and Eldon Square.[12] Within the new town some insensitive alterations and a degree of demolition behind retained facades reduced the full majesty of the original design but the vast proportion of the great scheme survived remarkably intact.

Of Grainger's major buildings, fire forced the not unwelcome rebuilding

**Eldon Square,
December 1972**

Considerable neglect and decay had taken its toll on Eldon Square by the 1960s. A decision to demolish it had been taken in 1964, although it was the construction of the new shopping centre which triggered its removal in 1973. At the time two arguments put forward for its demolition were that the town had plenty of other Grainger-Dobson related architecture and that "it is only the buildings surrounding the square that will be removed."

of the whole interior of the Theatre Royal from 1899 to 1901. Fire al created the opportunity for the formation of the Central Arcade within t Central Exchange complex in 1906, illustrating that it was possible introduce new elements to the area which enhanced rather than despoil Grainger's work. A further fire also led to the rebuilding of part of Grainge great market. But the loss of Eldon Square and the Royal Arcade cut deep into the city's pride, the backlash from which, together with the increasi national emphasis on the conservation of historic buildings and townscape fostered a new attitude to the rich architectural legacy of the city. T intensive programme of stone cleaning which took place in the 1970s help to return some of the architectural grandeur to Grainger's streets. Howev bringing contemporary commercial activity and residential life once more the area required a far more complex and long-term approach.

The "Grainger Town Project" established in 1993 by Newcastle C Council and its partners, English Partnerships and English Heritage, response to this challenge has developed a regeneration approach to tack symptoms of decline and to breathe new life into Grainger's new town a the surrounding area.[13] Recognising the growing amount of vaca floorspace, the rapid turnover of occupiers, the traffic congestion, limit parking, the declining standards of the streetscape and the lack of investme and interest in the area from both developers and occupiers of the buildin the Project team have developed a vision and a programme to take Graing Town into the new millennium. The vision for the Grainger Town area is th it will become a dynamic and competitive location in the heart of the Ci

**The Royal Arcade in the 1950s**

Having been in decline for many decades the Royal Arcade was a regular target for proposals of demolition. In the end the building was removed in stages from 1963 to 1969 to meet the needs of the new Pilgrim Street roundabout and office block. Despite its seeming redundancy the loss of the Arcade and the demolition of Eldon Square shortly afterwards were significant factors in the drive for the future conservation and renovation of Grainger's legacy.

that it will develop its role in the regional economy, within a high quality environment appropriate to a major European Regional Capital. Its reputation for excellence will be focused on leisure, culture and the arts and entrepreneurial activity. Grainger Town will become a distinctive place, a safe and attractive location to work, live and visit. To achieve this aim the project seeks to enhance employment prospects, support new and existing businesses, protect and improve the environment, promote good design and landscaping and improve residential properties. The key programmes established to achieve these goals look to broaden the area's economic base; to secure investment in a range of uses – office, housing, retail, arts and leisure which, in turn, it is hoped will lead to the repair and re-use of historic buildings; to increase the residential population of the area through the creation of affordable housing; to provide employment opportunities for youth and long-term unemployed within the area; and to market and promote the area to encourage the wide range of proposed activities. A combination of private and public funds will, it is hoped, be the catalyst, as Richard Grainger was, almost two centuries ago, to the successful reanimation and regeneration of the town centre which Richard Grainger built.

"This splendid series of streets bursts, in all the blaze of metropolitan grandeur, upon the eye … the buildings are spacious and lofty, their light and beautiful appearance is enhanced by the stone frontages, in which architectural grace blends with the stability of the mason's work."

(W. Caspey, 1846.)

*"Under the magic hand of a Grainger
a City of Palaces had suddenly sprung up."*

(From a speech at the opening of the Grainger Market,
October 22nd, 1835.)

# Notes

**Preface**

1. W. Howitt, *Visits to Remarkable Places*, 1842, p.310

**Introduction**

1. Report of Cholera Inquiry Commissioners, 1854, Newcastle upon Tyne, Evidence of Richard Grainger 26th January 1854

2. W. Lawson, *Tyneside Celebrities*, Newcastle upon Tyne, 1873

**Chapter One**

1. Raymond Williams, *The Country and the City*, Hogarth Press, London, 1985 p.9

2. Oliver Goldsmith, *The Deserted Village* (1770), Goldsmith Press, Ireland 1978 p.21 & p.38

3. See the Wessex novels of Thomas Hardy, particularly *Under The Greenwood Tree*, *The Mayor of Casterbridge* and *Tess of the D'Urbevilles*

4. George Elliot, *The Mill on the Floss*, 1860

5. Asa Briggs, *Victorian Cities*, Penguin Books, 1990 p.59

6. David Lowenthal, *The Past is a Foreign Country*, Cambridge University Press, 1985, p.96

7. Peter Mathias, *The First Industrial Nation*, London, 1969, p.228

8. T.S. Ashton, *Economic Fluctuations in England 1700-1800*, Oxford, 1959 – quoted in Mathias, op. cit.

9. Mathias, op. cit., p.236

10. John Smith, "Public Health on Tyneside, 1850-1880" in *Essays in Tyneside Labour History*, 1976 p.36

11. Lowenthal, op cit, p.97

12. Llewellyn Woodward, *The Age of Reform*, England 1815-1870, Oxford University Press,1962, pp.529-530

**Chapter Two**

1. Briggs, op. cit p.18

2. ibid p.33

3. ibid p.86

4. ibid p.140

5. ibid pp.364-5. The reference to bells ringing, clocks striking etc. dates from as far back as 1771

6. ibid p.365

7. ibid p.67

8. ibid p.75

9. ibid p.89. This observation, as Briggs points out, was made by a man from, "of all places Rotherham"

**Chapter Three**

1. Ian Ayris "Elemore Colliery and the Hetton Coal Company", Industrial Archaeology Review, Winter 1979-80, Vol IV, No.1 p.7

2. See Ian Ayris and Stafford Linsley, *A Guide to the Industrial Archaeology of Tyne and Wear*, Newcastle City Council, 1994

3. A reference, like many, attributable to Professor Norman McCord

4. Briggs, op. cit. p.37

5. G. Bennett, E. Clavering, A. Rounding, *A Fighting Trade, Rail Transport in Tyne Coal 1600-1800*, Gateshead, 1990, Vol 1, p.26

6. N. McCord, "Some Aspects of North East England in the Nineteenth Century", Northern History, VII (1972) pp73-88, also see D.J. Rowe "The Culleys, Northumberland Farmers 1767-1813", Agricultural History Review XIX (1971) pp156-174 and Phoebe Lowery "Patronage and the Country House in Northumberland", in *Northumbrian Panorama*, Octavian Press 1996, pp.49-73

7. N. McCord, op.cit. p.81, also see N. McCord "The Government of Tyneside 1800 -1850", Transactions of the Roy Historical Society (5) Vol. 20 (1970) p.5-30

8. Briggs, op.cit. p.373

9. See "Newcastle Acts and Byelaws", Reid 1888, an introduction by J.F.Gibson

10. J. Smith, op.cit. p.25

11. ibid p.26

12. ibid p.28

13. Woodward op.cit. p.463

14. Proceedings of Newcastle Town Council, Minutes February 7th 1838

15. J. Smith, op.cit. p.35

**Chapter Four**

1. Briggs, op.cit. p.110

2. I. Ayris and P. Sheldon, *On the Waterfront*, Newcastle City Libraries and Arts, 1995, p.15

3. See W. Boyd, Plan of Newcastle upon Tyne, 1909

4. L.F. Pearson, *Northern City: An Architectural History of Newcastle upon Tyne*, Newcastle City Libraries, 1996, p.16

5. Quoted in Lyall Wilkes, *Tyneside Portraits – Studies in Art and Life*, Frank Graham, 1971 p.108

6. ibid. p.109

7. Celia Fiennes, quoted in Pearson, op.cit. title page

8. R.J. Buswell, "Newcastle in the 16th and 17th Centuries" in *Newcastle's Changing Map*, Newcastle City Libraries & Arts, 1992, p.19

9. Henry Bourne, The History of Newcastle upon Tyne (1736). Reprinted 1980, p.126. See also Ayris & Sheldon, op. cit. p.7

10. See Pearson, op. cit

11. ibid p.18

12. M. Sill, "The Growth of Newcastle in the 18th and Early 19th Centuries" in *Newcastle's Changing Map*, p.25

13. Gentleman's Magazine, January 1807,p.38-39

**Chapter Five**

1. *Newcastle Courant* 2nd February 1811

2. *Newcastle Courant* 2nd March 1811

3. *Newcastle Advertiser* 1st April 1813

4. *Newcastle Courant* 16th March 1813

5. *Newcastle Advertiser* 18th May 1814

6. *Newcastle Courant* 1st April 1815

7. *Newcastle Courant* 29th March 1817

8. W. Gray, *Chorographia*, 1649, reprint Frank Graham, 1971

9. Bourne, op. cit. p.85

10. L. Wilkes & G. Dodds, *Tyneside Classical*, John Murray, London 1964, p.17

. *Newcastle Courant* 7th January 1826

**Chapter Six**

E. McKenzie, *A Descriptive and Historical Account of the Town and County of Newcastle upon Tyne*, 1827, Vol 1. p.172

Unpublished MSS notes of Mrs Suzanne Corbett of New Zealand to whom thanks are extended

St Andrew's Parish Baptism Register, Northumberland County Record Office

*Penny Magazine*, April 11th 1840

See S. Middlebrook, *Newcastle upon Tyne: its growth and achievement*, 2nd ed. 1968 p.120

T. Oliver, *A New Picture of Newcastle upon Tyne*, 1831, 127

McKenzie, op.cit.Vol 1 p.188

Wilkes & Dodds, op.cit. p.26-27

**Chapter Seven**

Oliver, op.cit. p.97

McKenzie, op.cit.Vol 1 p.188-189

Oliver, op. cit. p.96

W. Fordyce, *Historical Register of Remarkable Events*, 1829, p.244-5

*Penny Magazine*, April 11th 1840

ibid, April 11th 1840

ibid, April 11th 1840

ibid, April 11th 1840

See Pearson, op. cit. p. 21

**Chapter Eight**

T.E. Faulkner, "The Early Nineteenth Century Planning of Newcastle upon Tyne" Planning Perspectives 5 (1990) pp.152-3

T.F. Dibdin, *A Bibliographical, Antiquarian and Picturesque Tour in the Northern Counties of England*, London, 1838, p.365

ibid, p.366-7

*Newcastle Journal* 14th June 1834

Fordyce, op. cit. entry 15th July 1834

**Chapter Nine**

Fordyce, op. cit. entry July 30th 1834

*Penny Magazine*, April 18th 1840

ibid, April 18th 1840

Wilkes & Dodds, op.cit. p.82

Howitt, op. cit. p.311

*Penny Magazine*, May 9th 1840

*Newcastle Journal* 28th May 1836

ibid. 2nd June 1837

Proceedings, Oct 27th 1836

. *Newcastle Journal* 23rd June 1838

. Proceedings, Feb 7th 1838

. Pearson, op. cit. p.25

. Wilkes & Dodds, op.cit. p.130 f

. Proceedings, September 6th, 1837

. Collections relating to Newcastle, Newcastle City Library, ol 4, 817

. Proceedings, Special Meeting, Wed. September 14th 1836

17. ibid

18. I. Ayris, P. Jubb, S. Palmer, P. Usherwood, *A Guide to the Public Monuments and Sculpture of Tyne and Wear*, Newcastle City Council, 1996, p.12

19. P. Jubb. pers. comment

20. Proceedings, March 2nd 1837

21. *Penny Magazine*, March 9th, 1840

22. L. Wilkes, "The Grainger and Clayton Transformation" in *The Changing Face of Newcastle*, City of Newcastle, p.28

23. Howitt, op.cit. p.324

**Chapter Ten**

1. See Graingerised version of R. Welford, *Men of Mark Twixt Tyne and Tweed*, London, 1895, p.324

2. *Tyneside Portraits*, p.110

3. Lowenthal, op.cit. p.101

4. ibid p.99 – note also footnote reference to E. Trotman, "On the Alleged Degeneracy of Modern Architecture" (1834)

5. Report of Cholera Inquiry Commissioners, 26th January 1854

6. Proceedings, 1861

7. Collections Relating to Newcastle Vol 5, no. 1179

8. Report of Cholera Inquiry Commissioners, 26th January 1854

9. ibid

10. *Penny Magazine* April 18th 1840

11. Wilkes & Dodds, op. cit. p.82

12. *Newcastle Journal*, November 14th 1835

13. T. Faulkner & A. Greg, *John Dobson – Newcastle Architect 1787-1865*, Tyne & Wear Museums, 1987, p.46-7

14. Foundation stone laid 25th June 1835

15. H. Colvin, *A Biographical Dictionary of British Architects, 1600-1840*, John Murray, 1978, p.593

16. *Newcastle Journal* 4th July 1835

17. *Newcastle Journal* 24th March 1838

18. Howitt, op. cit. p.309

19. N. Pevsner, *The Buildings of England: Northumberland*, Penguin 1992, p.487

20. W.E. Gladstone Diary Entry 7th October 1862, quoted in Wilkes & Dodds, op.cit. p.79

21. Wilkes & Dodds, op. cit. p.89

**Chapter Eleven**

1. Mathias op. cit. p.236

2. See also T.P. McDermott "Irish Workers on Tyneside in the Nineteenth Century" in Essays in Tyneside Labour History, 1977, p.154-178

3. Proceedings, February 7th 1838

4. Sir Walter Besant quoted in Briggs, op. cit. p.24

5. See Wilkes & Dodds, op. cit. p.143

5. See Wilkes & Dodds, op. cit. for more information on the life and importance of John Clayton

6. C.C. Taylor & R.J. Buswell, "The Development of Central Newcastle" in *Newcastle's Changing Map*, p.31

7. Wilkes & Dodds, op. cit. p.71

8. Faulkner, op. cit. p. 154. See also Taylor & Buswell, op. cit. p.31

9. Proceedings, Letter from Richard Grainger, 4 October 1837

10. Seymour Bell papers, Newcastle City Library, Elswick Estate, 8

11. T. Faulkner & P. Lowery, *Lost Houses of Newcastle and Northumberland*, Jill Raines, 1996, p.17

12. Clayton-Gibson correspondence books, Tyne & Wear Archives, 39

13. ibid, November 26th 1839

14. ibid, November 26th 1839

15. Wilkes & Dodds, op. cit. p.109

16. Clayton-Gibson, October 6th 1841

17. ibid, October 6th 1841

18. ibid, December 31st 1841

19. ibid, December 31st 1841

20. ibid, October 16th 1841

21. For an explanation of the complexities of the arrangement see Wilkes & Dodds, op. cit. pp.115-121

22. Wilkes & Dodds, op. cit. p.119

## Chapter Twelve

1. *Penny Magazine*, May 9th 1840

2. Dibdin, op. cit. p.365

3. Collections relating to Newcastle VI/1398

4. Wilkes & Dodds, op. cit. p.143

5. Collections relating to Newcastle V/2 Handbill, December 24th 1835

6. *Penny Magazine*, May 9th 1840

7. See Rennison, R.W., *Water to Tyneside*, 1979, for a detailed description of Grainger's involvement in the water supply industry

8. *Penny Magazine*, May 9th 1840

9. Proceedings, Letter of 4th October 1837

10. Lord Clive (of India) replying to accusations of corruption during Parliamentary cross-examination, 1773

11. Tyne & Wear Archives ref D/NCP/4/45 & 46. Also see Wilkes & Dodds, op. cit., p.142

12. Obituary Notice, Town Council Proceedings, July 1861

13. ibid

14. *Penny Magazine*, April 11th 1840

15. Some sources give this number as fifteen, but the most authoritative source is A. J. Pain, "The Grainger Family of Newcastle" in *Northumberland and Durham Family History Society Journal*, Vol 5, No. 4, (July 1980) p.94-95 which records thirteen children

16. See Wilkes & Dodds, op. cit. p.143

17. Notes prepared and generously given to the Grainger Town Project by Mrs L. Rosbottom of Yeovil, Somerset, a surviving descendant of the Grainger family through Richard Grainger's daughter Juliet Isabella

18. Wilkes & Dodds, op. cit. p.119

19. *Newcastle Daily Journal* – August 18th 1868. I am indebted to Trish Sheldon of Newcastle City Library for this reference

20. Ayris, Jubb, Palmer & Usherwood, op. cit. p.37

21. *Newcastle Daily Journal*, 5th July 1861

22. *The Daily Chronicle and Northern Counties Advertiser*, 11th July 1861, quoted in Faulkner, op. cit. p.167

23. *Newcastle Journal*, quoted in Wilkes & Dodds, op. cit., p. 78

## Chapter Thirteen

1. Faulkner & Greg, op. cit. p. 48

2. Smith, op. cit. p.36

3. ibid, p.25

4. Ayris & Sheldon, op. cit. p.25

5. see McCord, op. cit.

6. Quoted in Ayris & Sheldon, op. cit. p.29

7. Proceedings, September 6th 1837

8. See T. E. Faulkner "Conservation and Renewal in Newcastle upon Tyne" in *Northumbrian Panorama*, 123-145 and *Newcastle's Changing Map* for more detailed information on the late nineteenth and twentieth century development of the city centre

9. Pevsner, op. cit. p.485

10. J. B. Priestley, *English Journey*, (1934) Heinneman 1984, p.219-234

11. See Faulkner, "Conservation and Renewal in Newcastle upon Tyne" op. cit. p. 134 -140

12. ibid. p. 141-144

13. EDAW, *Graingertown Regeneration Strategy*, Newcastle City Council, 1996

# ndex

| | |
|---|---|
| bert Edward Dock | 16, 77p |
| bert Edward, Prince of Wales | 77p |
| lhusen, Christian | 65 |
| nderson, George | 30 |
| nderson, Major | 30, 40 |
| nderson Place | 28, 29p, 30p, 40, 41, 44, 63 |
| nderson, Robert | 29, 30 |
| chitecture – Newcastle | 53-58 |
| mstrong, William | 65, 73, 77 |
| undale, Joseph | 33, 72 |
| undale, Rachel | See Grainger, Rachel |
| ainbridge's | 59 |
| rras Bridge | 27 |
| tson, Alderman William | 32, 34, 62 |
| gg Market | 14p, 42, 48, 63 |
| rmingham | 13 |
| ackett, Sir William | 29, 30, 32 |
| ackett Street | 7, 34, 35, 36, 40, 41, 42, 79 |
| ake, William | 12 |
| andford Street | 75 |
| enheim Street | 75 |
| ourne, Henry | 23 |
| adford | 10, 13, 14 |
| andling Place | 24 |
| own, John | 32 |
| owning, Robert | 12 |
| urdon, Thomas | 27 |
| urns, Rachel Elizabeth | 73, 74 |
| urt, Thomas | 31 |
| arliol Street | 7, 33 |
| entral Exchange | 48, 49p, 56, 57, 58p, 58, 63, 65, 76, 80 |
| entral Station | 75, 78 |
| harlotte Square | 24 |
| hemical Industry | 16 |
| holera | 11, 22, 76 |
| holera Commission | 55 |
| avering Place | 22 |
| ayton, John | 34, 40, 43, 53, 59, 61, 62, 65, 66, 67, 70, 71, 73 |
| ayton, Nathaniel | 24, 61 |
| ayton Street | 7, 42, 43, 48, 54p, 56 |
| ayton Street West | 7, 66 |
| ose, The | 22 |
| oal Industry | 10, 13, 16, 17p |
| oal Trade | 16, 17, 27 |
| oleridge, Samuel Taylor | 12 |
| ollingwood Street | 25, 28, 41, 78 |
| onstruction Industry | 11, 59, 60 |
| orn Exchange | 37, 39, 41, 48, 61, 62p, 63 |
| ourt Proposal | 48, 57, 58, 61, 63 |
| oft Street | 7 |
| ean Street | 24, 25, 29, 41, 51p, 77 |
| efoe, Daniel | 22 |
| ickens, Charles | 12 |
| obson, John | 27, 28p, 3437, 44, 49, 50, 54, 75 |
| ublin | 55 |
| onomic climate | 11, 27, 59 |
| inburgh | 55, 78 |
| don Square | 7, 34-36, 39, 41, 42, 79, 80, 80p |
| Eliot, George | 10 |
| Ellison Place | 24, 28 |
| Elswick Hall | 64-66 |
| Elswick Estate | 7, 63p, 64, 67-70 |
| Exeter | 14, 18 |
| Fenwick, John | 34, 36, 61, 62 |
| Fenwick's Store | 77, 78p |
| Fiennes, Celia | 22 |
| Forth Banks | 27 |
| French Revolution | 10 |
| Gateshead | 79 |
| Gibson, William | 73 |
| Glass Industry | 16 |
| Goldsmith, Oliver | 9 |
| Grainger, Amelia | 31, 71 |
|    Amelia Jnr | 31 |
|    George | 31, 32 |
|    Henry Benjamin | 71 |
|    John | 31 |
|    Joseph | 71 |
|    Rachel | 33, 62, 71, 72p |
|    Thomas Charles | 66, 71 |
|    William | 31 |
| Grainger, Richard | |
|    Achievements | 7, 8 |
|    Architect | 55 |
|    Blackett Street | 35, 36 |
|    Character | 68, 69 |
|    Death | 71, 73, 74 |
|    Early Years | 31-34 |
|    Eldon Square | 35-36, 39 |
|    Elswick adventure | 61-66 |
|    Family | 31-33, 71, 72 |
|    Financial dealings | 61-66 |
|    Influences upon | 59-62 |
|    Leazes Terrace | 36, 37, 39 |
|    Legacy | 75-83 |
|    Memorials to | 73 |
|    Political views | 69, 69p |
|    Portraits | 6, 8, 67 |
|    Royal Arcade | 37-39 |
|    Town Centre Work | 40-58 |
|    Will | 66, 68, 71 |
| Grainger Street | 7, 42, 43, 45, 48, 52p, 56, 74 |
| Grainger St. West | 56p, 61, 71, 75, 77 |
| Grainger Town Project | 80, 81 |
| Graingerville South | 65 |
| Green, John & Benjamin | 32, 49, 54, 57 |
| Grey, Earl | 49 |
| Grey's Monument | 49, 50, 50p, 57, 74 |
| Grey Street | 7, 41, 42, 48-51, 53p, 56-58, 74p, 77, 78, 82p, 83p |
| Groat Market | 42, 63 |
| Hanover Square | 22 |
| Hardy, Thomas | 9 |
| Harvest failure | 11 |
| High Bridge | 48 |
| High Friar Lane | 31, 32p |
| High Level Bridge | 70p, 71, 75, 77, 78 |
| Higham Place | 32, 33p |
| Hinde, John Hodgson | 64 |
| Hodgson, John | 64 |
| Hood Street | 7, 42, 55-57 |
| Howitt, William | 51, 58 |

| | |
|---|---|
| Industrialisation | 9, 13 |
| Iron Industry | 16p |
| | |
| Jacobite Rising | 20 |
| Jesmond | 27 |
| John Dobson Street | 79 |
| | |
| King Street | 76 |
| | |
| Lombard Street | 76 |
| Leazes Crescent | 7, 36, 40 |
| Leazes Terrace | 34, 36, 37p, 39, 70 |
| Leeds | 10, 13, 14 |
| Liddell, Henry | 71 |
| Lincoln | 14 |
| Liverpool | 13 |
| London | 13, 14, 16, 55, 78 |
| Lort Burn | 41, 45 |
| | |
| Manchester | 10, 13, 14-16 |
| Manor Chare | 38 |
| Markets, Butcher (old) | 42, 45, 47 |
|    Grainger | 45, 46p, 47p, 47, 56, 57, 80 |
|    Medieval | 14, 59 |
| Market Street | 7, 42, 47, 49, 56, 57, 70, 78 |
| Martineau, Harriet | 33, 40, 45, 50, 68 |
| McKenzie, Eneas | 35, 76 |
| Methodism | 32, 34, 62 |
| Middle Street | 37, 63 |
| Middlesbrough | 13 |
| Mosley Street | 24, 25, 28, 29, 34, 37, 41, 48, 78 |
| Municipal Reform Act | 17 |
| | |
| Napoleonic Wars | 7, 11, 27 |
| Nelson Street | 7, 42, 56 |
| Neville Street | 42, 48 |
| New Bridge Street | 7, 33, 78 |
| Newcastle | |
|    Corporation | 17, 19, 35, 40, 43, 44, 49, 61, 63, 65, 66, 71 |
|    Changes since Grainger | 75-83 |
|    Economic Conditions | 14, 59 |
|    Quayside | 18, 18p, 20, 76, 76p |
|    Regional Capital | 16 |
|    Residential Development | 23, 24, 27, 28 |
|    Social Condition | 18, 19, 23, 36, 75, 76 |
|    Town Centre Development | 41-50 |
|    Town Walls | 20, 20p, 21, 34 |
|    Water Supply | 18 |
| Newgate Street | 7, 32, 42, 75 |
| Nicholson, Peter | 57 |
| North Shields | 24, 49 |
| North Shore | 24 |
| Northern Academy of Fine Arts | 35 |
| Northumberland Dock | 16 |
| Northumberland Street | 7, 77-79 |
| Norwich | 14 |
| Nun Street | 7, 42 |
| Nuns Fields | 28, 30, 40-42 |
| Nun's Gate | 7 |
| | |
| Oliver, Andrew | 54, 57 |
| Oliver, Thomas | 34-37, 40, 41, 49, 52, 54, 57 |
| Ouseburn | 24 |
| | |
| Pandon Dean | 27 |
| Percy Street | 7, 28, 32, 33, 42, 75 |
| | |
| Philadelphia | 15 |
| Pilgrim Street | 7, 34, 37, 38, 42, 44p, 48, 7 |
| Plague | 22 |
| Population | 10, 22, 60 |
| Portland Place | 7 |
| Pottery Industry | 16 |
| Priestley, J.B. | 78 |
| | |
| Quayside | 18, 18p, 76, 76p, 77 |
| Queen Street | 76 |
| | |
| Railway Street | 7 |
| Railways | 13, 75 |
| Royal Arcade | 7, 34, 37-39, 43, 79-81p |
| Ruskin, John | 14 |
| Rye Hill | 7 |
| | |
| St Andrew's Church | 31, 34 |
| St Andrew's Parish School | 32 |
| St James' Street | 7 |
| St James' Terrace | 7 |
| St Mary's Place | 36 |
| Salt Industry | 16, 24 |
| Saville Row | 24 |
| Scott, Sir Walter | 12 |
| Seven Dials Circus | 41, 42, 49 |
| Shakespeare Street | 7, 42, 57 |
| Shipbuilding | 16 |
| Side, The | 25, 26p |
| Steel Industry | 13 |
| Stephenson, David | 24, 42, 54 |
| Stephenson, George | 73, 74 |
| Stephenson, Robert | 73 |
| Stokoe, William | 24, 64 |
| Storey, John | 9 |
| | |
| Tennyson, Alfred Lord | 12 |
| Textile Industry | 10, 13 |
| Theatre Royal (old) | 42, 43p, 45, 46 |
| Theatre Royal ( new) | 47, 57, 58, 80 |
| Trafalgar, Battle of | 27 |
| Turk's Head Inn (old) | 46 |
| Turk's Head Inn (new) | 47, 58 |
| Turnpike Roads | 21, 24 |
| Tyne Bridge | |
|    Medieval | 21p |
|    Georgian | 22p, 65 |
|    Twentieth Century | 44, 78 |
| Tyne Dock | 16 |
| | |
| Victoria, Queen | 78 |
| | |
| Wakefield | 14 |
| Walker, George | 56, 57 |
| Wallsend | 17p, 79 |
| Wardle, John | 56, 57 |
| Waterloo, Battle of | 7 |
| Westgate Road/Street | 25, 42, 48 |
| Wilkes, Judge Lyall | 50 |
| Wordsworth, William | 12 |
| | |
| York | 14 |